To Eric
with many thanks
Sincerely

Karl Menninger
Scarsdale
Jan. 14. 1982.

The Spirit of Man: The Sculpture of Kaare Nygaard

The Spirit of Man: The Sculpture of Kaare Nygaard

Text by Nathan Cabot Hale
Photographs by Amy Binder

Medical Arts Publishing Foundation
Dreyer

TO THE MEMORY OF TWO GOOD WOMEN
MY MOTHER, MY WIFE.

                              KKN

DESIGNER: ULRICH RUCHTI

DESIGN ASSISTANT: LESLIE ROSENBERG

TEXT EDITOR: JOAN L. POOLE

ISBN-0-292-77575-X USA

ISBN-82-09-101234 NORGE

List of Works

Nietzsche	9, 11
Dostoevski	12
Young Litteratus	15 16
Sketch after El Greco	17
Old Abe	20, 22, 23
Girl with Norweigian Cap	24, 25
Lady with Norwegian Cap	26, 27
Little Elizabeth	28
Me at 1 year Old, self-portrait	30, 32, 33
My Friend, the Stallion Herdsman	34, 35
Dr. Ben Colcock	36, 37
Hamlet, figure	38, 39
Hamlet, head	40, 41
Spirit of Dance—Martha Graham	42, 43
The English Barrister	44
My Friend, the Village Idiot	46, 47, 48, 49
Father of the Village Idiot	50, 51
Lady with Large Hat	52, 53
The Poet and Pegasus	54, 55
Grazing Horse	57
Freedom Fighter up against the Wall	59, 61
Viet Nam	62, 63
Caveman	64, 65
Concentration Camp Inmate—Hunger	66, 67
Fever	68, 69
The Art critic	70
The Museum Director	72, 73
Ultimatum	74, 76, 77
Exodus	78, 79, 80
In the Sweat of Your Brow Shall You Earn Your Bread	82, 84, 85
Pietà	86, 87, 88
Hour of Meditation	90, 91
The Borgia Pope	93, 94, 95
The Musician	97
Homage to Paul Gauguin	98, 99, 101
Homage to Vincent Van Gogh	102, 103
Homage to Vincent Van Gogh	104, 105
Rodin	107
Percy Grainger, Pianist, Composer, Musical Genius	108, 111
Marcel Duchamp	112, 113, 114
Joseph Hirshhorn	117, 118
The Drunkard	120, 121
Seated Moses	122, 123
Standing Moses	124, 125
The Virgin Mary	126, 127

Hiroshima   129, 130, 131
Men Against Man   132, 133
The Death of Savonarola   134, 136, 137
Cancer   138, 139, 140, 141
Monument for Knut Hamsun,
   Norwegian Nobel Prize Winner for Literature   142, 143, 144
Edvard Munch, head   146, 148
Edvard Munch, after Self-Portrait   151
Ambivalence, Edvard Munch   152, 153, 154
In Memoriam   156, 157

Foreword

Dr. Kaare K. Nygaard is a born recreator. As a master surgeon, superbly trained, he not only saved lives with his consummate skill and sensitive hands, but he saved people—not only by healing their wounds but by helping them to remold their psyche.

Now his almost extrasensory hands have made images of personalities in clay and precious metals for all to see. One must feel, awesomely, viewing his masterpieces, that there are two priceless ingredients. The first is love; the second is compassion. To which might be added a no small talent for art and sculptural endeavors.

HOWARD A. RUSK, M.D.
Distinguished University Professor
New York University

Introduction

I was introduced to the sculpture of K. K. Nygaard by my old friend, the distinguished photographer of sculpture David Finn. David also happens to be the father of Amy Binder, the talented photographer of this book. Though Mr. Finn had told me something about Nygaard's background as a surgeon and his devotion to his avocation of sculpture, I was a bit sceptical about what this combination of medical experience and art might produce. I recalled a certain expression on the face of Jacques Lipshitz when he spoke of "doctor's sculpture." I only knew that Mr. Finn thought a book should be done and that I trusted his judgment in matters of art. But I was frankly curious whether I would find a point of departure that would make it possible for me to write about this surgeon who was also a sculptor.

My writing on art is based on the fact that I am myself a professional sculptor who has worked at the craft for close to forty years. It is also defined by the academic work that I have done in the field of morphology as it relates to the psychology of human imagery. These two factors limit my writing to those aspects of figurative art that I feel need clarification for either the profession or the public. This meant that Nygaard's work had to be more than just interesting to me; it had to express something that I considered worth talking about.

My first impression of Nygaard's work was that it had extraordinary expressive power, but at the same time many technical shortcomings. However, as a long-time teacher of figure modeling and artistic anatomy, I have always looked on technique as a means rather than an end. . . . What an artist says is usually more important than how he or she says it. All the technique in the world means nothing if an artist is not in contact with the emotional roots of human expression . . . and in Nygaard's case it was a matter of the artist's expressive drives outstripping his technical means. It seemed to me that Nygaard's work came into being solely by his will to express. And as I came to know his work and the factors of his development, I came to understand that it was always his drive to express his inner visions that drew him along the path of art . . . even into very difficult technical undertakings. At the beginning of my acquaintance with him,

there were two particular works that attracted my attention and convinced me that his sculpture was indeed worth writing about.

The first Nygaard sculpture to catch my eye was his portrait of Joseph Hirshhorn, the powerful financier, patron of artists, and founder of the Hirshhorn Museum in Washington, D.C., who was also Nygaard's patient and friend. I had been interested in Hirshhorn for many years because of the complexity of his character and because of his position of power and influence in art. Nygaard's portrait caught my eye before I even knew who the subject was. When I was told whom the portrait represented, it confirmed many of the qualities that I knew must exist in so complex a person as Hirshhorn, and I was impressed with Nygaard's perceptive depiction of those character traits. He was able to see things that are usually *invisible* to most people.

The second sculpture, Nygaard's *Men Against Man* also impressed me, but in a completely negative way. This work seemed to represent all of his technical deficiencies. I thought it was pompous, an altogether overstated stock "protest" work. I felt it was particularly odious and found it inexplicably irritating. It annoyed me to such an extent that I began to wonder at the strength of my own reaction. The work depicts a tightly packed group of lumpish, uniformed figures forcibly restraining one naked and pitifully struggling human figure. The irritation this work caused me was painful, but at the same time, something in it nagged at my consciousness. After a certain time, the reason for my urge to reject this image came out . . . certain memories returned to me.

Twice in my life I have had the dubious distinction of finding myself suddenly under the power of armed, lawless, mindless men in jackboots, uniforms, and visored caps. I have the painful memory of such men coming at me with upraised truncheons, have felt their blows, suffered their degradation, and experienced the appalling terror that I might not survive the next few minutes. These are not memories one tries to keep in the conscious mind; they are memories that one strives to make invisible. Nygaard's sculpture brought these memories back to me, and they caused me pain because he had clearly depicted the

whole monstrous, terrorizing theme. The sculpture said it exactly as it happens: the helplessness, the fear, the feelingless brutality. Once my own memories had reemerged, I began to truly appreciate the expressive genius of this sculpture. I knew then that I must attempt to write about these difficult human expressions that have emerged in Nygaard's sculpture because the understanding of these expressions is important to both figurative artists and the ordinary people who have been struggling to survive the difficulties of life in the twentieth century.

Once I realized *why* I must write about Nygaard's work, I was faced with the problem of *how* to write about it. His work was technically uneven and emotionally difficult. He is a literate, cultured man who has achieved eminence in medical science. However, though he grew up in a richly artistic environment, he has had no professional training in the rigorous techniques of sculpture, with the exception of his contacts with artists and being tutored in childhood. His lifelong love of art and his layman's study of it make him a theoretical sophisticate, while his lack of training makes him a technical primitive. His accumulated work ranges from his first tentative efforts to the ambitious large-scale pieces of his later years, and scattered among these are a few pieces that are works of expressive genius. His development was often uneven and his modeling unsure, yet overriding it all there is always a unique power of personal expression and a compassionate humanity. This unusual combination of factors has led me to label Nygaard a "self-taught" artist because what he has done he has done for reasons of his own.

Since the major element of his work is its expressive power, I have chosen to write about the factors in his origin, upbringing, his studies and work in the field of medicine that have produced his perceptive and expressive drives. The expressive force of Nygaard's work seems to have grown from the soil of his Norwegian heritage, his family life, and his lifelong devotion to his career in medicine rather than from the confused and dehumanized art movements of the twentiety century. Because of this, I have written about his learning and human insight gained as a medical man in contrast to the failure of twentieth-century art to cope with the real problems of the human image. When we see Nygaard's work in the light of these contrasts, it becomes possible for us to understand why he has seen aspects of life that often *seem* invisible to the average person.

Most important of all are the roots of his character and sensibility that were nurtured in the rich and warm Norwegian environment of his childhood and youth. Nygaard grew to manhood in a place and time that was kindly, decent, and humane. There was a beauty and simplicity in that place, there was a closeness to nature and an enjoyment of life, and there was music, painting, and sculpture. I have written about his origins because they tell us why he has cared so much about his fellow beings and why he has attempted to communicate with us in his sculpture.

I have purposely shunned any extended verbal discussion of Nygaard's work for several very substantial reasons. The first is that the artist's language of form and the language of words are always mysteriously incompatible. My task here is not to criticize Nygaard's work, but rather to indicate that the work itself has something of importance to tell us. If you learn nothing else from this book, there is one thing that I hope you will remember: *A work of art is itself an explanation.* The test of a work of art is that it communicates its own message. Because of this, Nygaard's work must stand on its own merits and speak to those who are willing or able to hear its message.

But there is still one further reason why I have limited my comments. In his photography of sculpture, David Finn, Amy Binder's father, has pioneered a new and important kind of relationship between photography and sculpture. This innovation has produced a means of leading the viewer in and around a sculpture in a way that is far closer to the sculptor's language of form than words. Amy Binder has worked with her father for a number of years, and in this book, she shows that she has herself become a skilled exponent of the photographic essay on the wordless language of sculpture. My comments only serve as a setting for these pictures, a placing in context. Once you have read my thoughts, let Nygaard's work speak for itself through these excellent pictures.

Young Litteratus, bronze, 13 × 9 × 5½

The Art of the Human Image

The life and sculpture of K. K. Nygaard reach to the very heart of the problems of twentieth-century figurative art, which may seem surprising to the reader because Nygaard, by his own definition, has been an avocational artist. During the greater part of his career as an artist, he has only been able to work for brief periods of time each day, while carrying out full-time responsibilities as a surgeon—and one of considerable reputation. More surprising is the fact that he has had no professional training in sculpture and is self-taught in every aspect of the craft. But limiting as his lack of formal training may seem, these very limitations have been the factors that have enabled him to draw from his own experience and insight far more real human expression than most formally trained artists. The pressing limitations on Nygaard's time and his self-education have produced an isolation and solitude that have enabled him to touch the expressive core of human problems that has been all but ignored by the twentieth-century art establishment. Nygaard's work has something important to say to us . . . something few twentieth-century artists have the experience or abililties to say.

In order for us to appreciate Nygaard's accomplishments as an artist, we must try to understand the creative conflicts that have so immobilized twentieth-century figurative art. And by the term "figurative art" we mean art that deals with deep human emotions, human expressions, and relationships in terms of the undistorted human image. The first of these conflicts has been generated by the academic debate about what qualifies a person to make artistic observations on human life. Who does have the right to create images of emotion, character, and facets of relationships between people? The simple answer to this is that making observations about life in words or images is a natural occupation practiced by almost everybody. Some people perceive more clearly than others, some people communicate more clearly than others. But it seems that this kind of communication is one of the most basic, natural human rights. Still, there are those who judge the value of artistic expressions more on the basis of the technical ability and academic training of the artist than on the content of what is said. The unfortunate thing about this viewpoint is that it tends to exclude self-taught artists from recognition . . . and quite often it is these very self-taught originals who have unique and new things to say to us. The fact remains, there has yet to be devised an art study program that could train artists to fathom the depths of the human soul.

One of the outstanding peculiarities of twentieth-century art training and theory—figurative or abstract—is its total exclusion of training in the skills of observation and delineation of human emotional expression, character development, and human inter-relationship. As a matter of fact, art has become increasingly nonhuman and abstract in form and content and is frequently completely devoid of human reference. In instances where human reference does occur, the human figure may be geometri-calized, fragmented, archaicized, violently distorted or—what yet may prove to be far more inhuman—politicized in the fashion of communist and fascist art. This predominant undercurrent of antihuman expression exists in the culture itself and may well have its roots in the mechanization of life functions and work by the economistic thinking that has taken over the mind of modern man.

In the field of art, neither the proponents of academic abstraction nor the proponents of academic realism have recognized the extent of their failure in human expression. They seem rather to place the blame on one another like Tweedle Dum and Tweedle Dee. The abstractionists hold the academic figure artists to be the villains who scorned Impressionism, drove Van Gogh to madness, and sent Gauguin to the South Seas. To the abstractionists, the academics are against all that is new, adventurous, and progressive. To them, art must always progress in a mechanistically forced distortion of the evolutionary process. But the remaining academics are no better; they claim riparian rights to the stream of art history itself. They own such great figures as Rembrandt and Rodin to be their progenitors, over-

Sketch after El Greco, bronze, 18 × 11 × 8

looking the fact that these artists were treated very shabbily by the academics of their day. Academic figurative artists go further and base their claims to righteousness on the fact that they are the bearers of traditional teaching values, and by this they mean their advocacy of teaching rigid anatomical construction, standardized painting and sculpture technique, and drawing from the bored posed model. But what has this to do with Nygaard?

Both the abstract and figurative schools have precious little human understanding or factual knowledge about human functioning. Nygaard, with his years of medical training, years of human observation, and years of dealing directly with serious human problems, has more genuine qualifications for making human statements in sculpture than most of the figurative artists of this century . . . simply because artists have abdicated the principle of rigorous study and human observation.

It is not intended here to claim that medical training in anatomy, pathology, and psychology is the royal road to training figurative artists. This is decidedly not true, and if it were true, every physician would be an automatically skilled artist, which is certainly not the case. Artistic anatomy is an independent discipline with a tradition and purpose that goes back hundreds (perhaps thousands) of years. Its purpose and techniques are completely different from medical anatomy, though there are some overlapping functions. The artistic study of the human figure is concerned with human form in relation to two- and three-dimensional form construction, the object of which is to delineate human expression, emotion, and character. Medical training in anatomy is structured in terms of physiological functions, pathology, and surgical procedure. Since the field of figurative art has abdicated deep and intensive human observation and the most profound aspects of human content in art, medical training is far closer to real study of the human figure than contemporary art training is. Though Nygaard has had no intensive training in drawing from the figure, artistic anatomy, or sculpture modeling technique, his experience, his human concern, and his aesthetic instincts are his very valid credentials.

Old Abe

Girl with Norwegian Cap, bronze, 16 × 10 × 10
Lady with Norwegian Cap, bronze, 24½ × 10 × 10, pp. 26, 27

Understanding the Form and Content of Human Imagery

The great difficulty in understanding human form and content in art stems from the confusion in art about what expression in a work of art really means. Understanding the function of expression in art has been obscured by promotion of the concept that the sole purpose of art is that the artist "express himself." This has confused the creation of art with psychiatrically induced emotional catharsis and has given the impression that the creation of art has to do only with the release of pent-up frustrations within the artist. In actuality, the function of figurative art is to allow the artist to create a work that is expressive of its human subject, one that is done with such skill that the work of art enables the viewer to understand and participate in the feeling of the subject depicted and develop a spiritual empathy with both the artist and subject. This kind of creation of "expressive works of art" has historically been the achievement of the great figurative artists of the past. Twentieth-century art has substituted "self-expression" and the concept of a compulsive and mechanistic "progress" for this very important function of figurative art. Nygaard has instinctively understood this.

The real problem of art is not to push compulsively beyond such artists as Rembrandt or Leonardo through the desperate creation of novelties but to strive to achieve some modicum of their human understanding and contact with nature. Twentieth-century art has lost contact with this purpose, but Nygaard has trustingly adhered to it in his isolation. He has naively striven to express humanly meaningful things and, in his naiveté, has seemed to comprehend instinctively human emotional content. But what is human emotional content, and why is it so difficult for artists to understand?

Human expression is difficult to understand because it is a layered psychic phenomenon that is full of seeming inconsistencies and contradictions. Human expressions are not simple expressions of one emotion or action, except in newborn infants. They are a layering of many emotions and actions. This layering of expression is difficult to understand, visualize, and depict because surface character traits usually hide the deeper ones. These deceptive character traits vary from very simple and trans-

parent ones to those that are all but impossible to penetrate. They range from simple control of emotional expression and bodily feeling to dissimulation, pretense, self-deception, intentional misdirection, outright fraud, and psychotic treachery. Underlying all these forms of surface defense is the real character of the person and his or her true emotions and qualities. And underneath *that* is the indefinable human essence we call the soul, which is so different and unique in every individual. Few artists have the intellectual capacity or emotional stamina to study human expression on its deepest levels.

By default of twentieth-century figurative art, physicians are better trained in the visual study of human beings than artists are. In figurative art education, there has been no effort to develop a curriculum that deals with anything beyond simple anatomy and figure drawing; there is no training in the forms of human expression, emotion, and the changing relationships and body language of life. These things are not only ignored, they are avoided. Nygaard's human insight and experience more than compensate for any lack of formal technical training.

For at least fifty years of his adult life, Nygaard has consistently practiced objective human observation. His daily work as a medical man has provided far more rigorous experience in observation than most figurative artists could even imagine. Day after day, year after year, Nygaard has observed and analyzed somewhere between twenty and forty patients a day. He has seen each of these people with full attention to their deepest states of being . . . and he has seen far more than medical facts . . . he has seen something of the human heart. Nygaard has something special within himself that has urged him to communicate the things that he felt so deeply about humanity. While practicing an extremely difficult profession, and achieving excellence in it, he has been pressed by some inner drive to communicate things to us in sculpture. Some inner drive has led him to attempt a very difficult program of self-teaching in art and has then led him through more than thirty years of creation in sculpture. During these years he has struggled to define human expressions that are extremely difficult to visualize and depict in art. And he has done this well. His friend Marcel Duchamp called Nygaard "the Sculptor of the Invisible" because of his masterful ability to make the elusive and intangible real and visible.

Me at 1 Year Old, self-portrait, bronze, 9 × 5 × 4, pp. 30, 32, 33

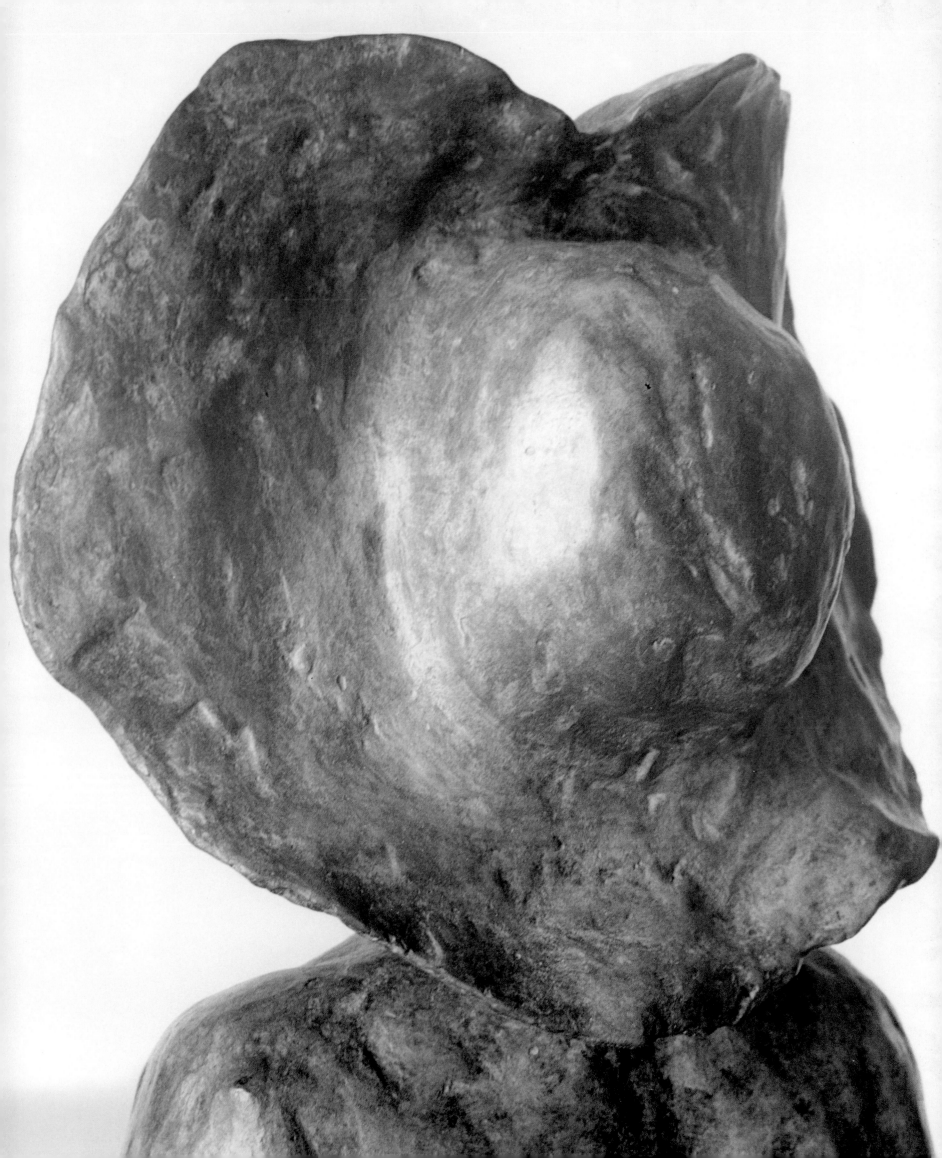

My Friend, the Stallion Herdsman, bronze, 23½ × 15 × 16½

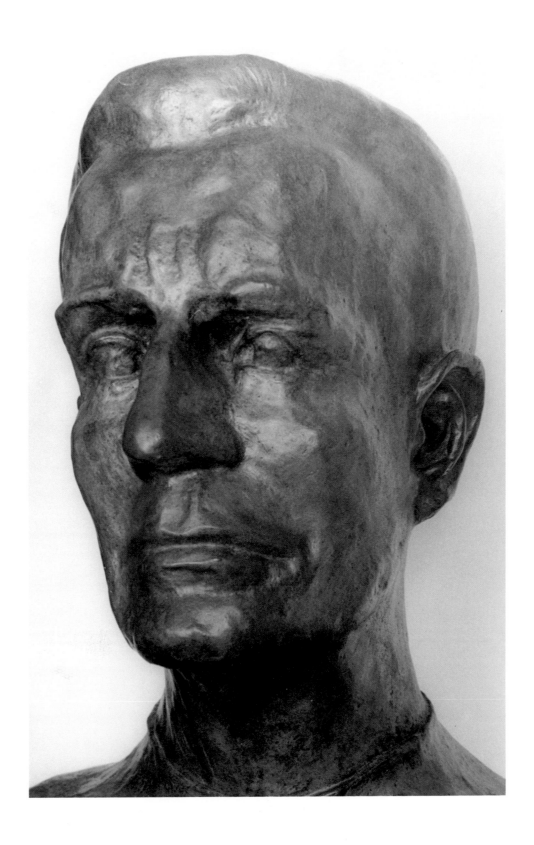

Dr. Ben Colcock, bronze, 21½ × 21 × 15
Hamlet, figure, bronze, 22½ × 5½ × 4½, pp. 38, 39
Hamlet, head, plaster of paris for bronze, 18½ × 14 × 9, pp. 40, 41
Spirit of Dance — Martha Graham, bronze, 58 × 69 × 24, pp. 42, 43

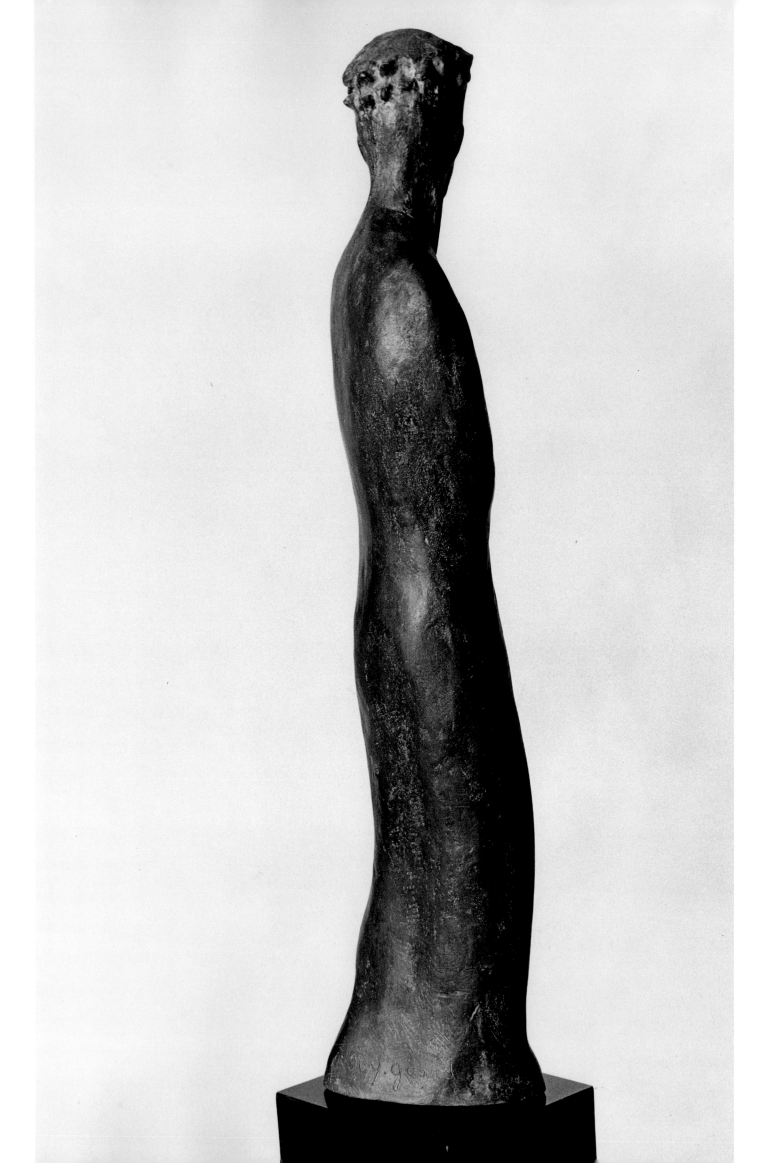

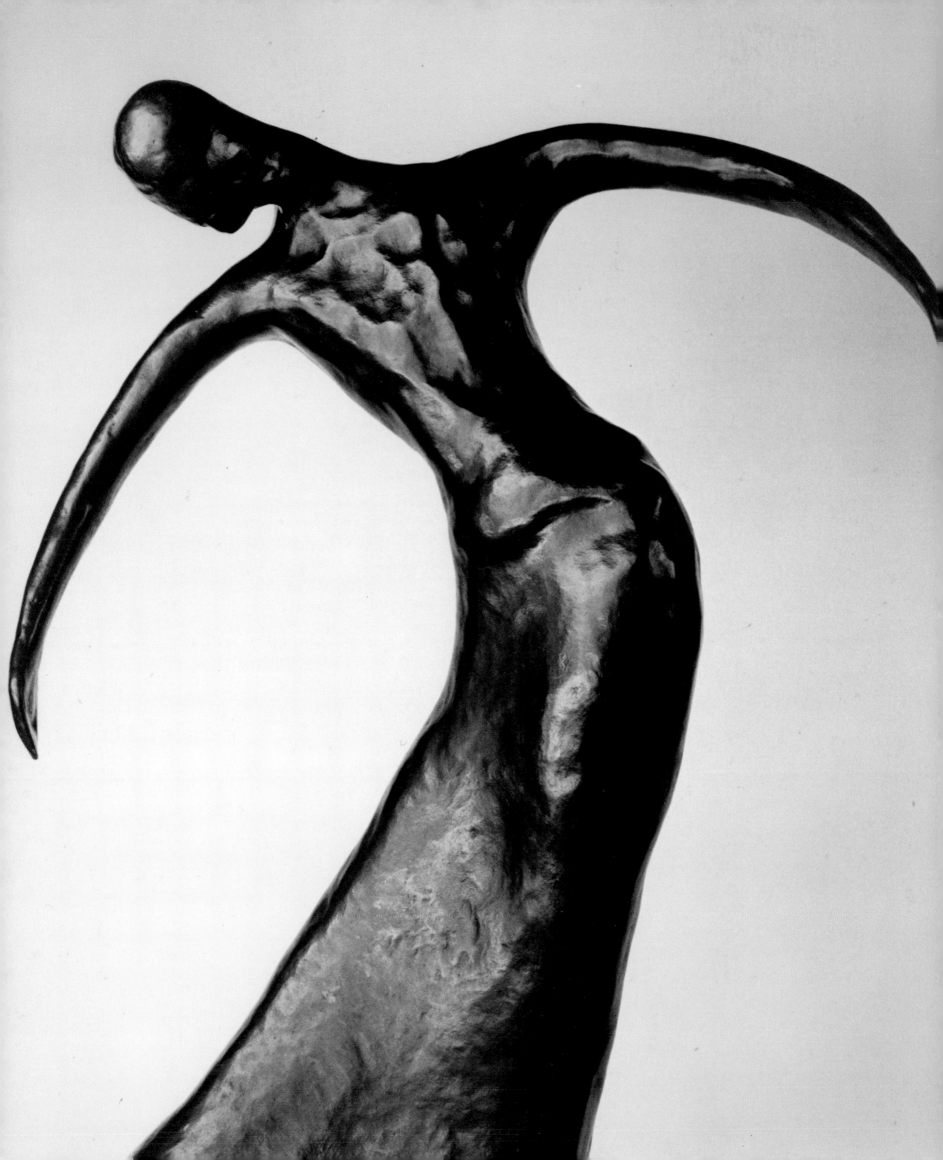

Some Biographical Facts on Nygaard

Kaare Kristian Nygaard was born in the town of Lillehammer in Norway. This town is located in the mountains, at the northern end of Norway's largest lake, and is about one hundred miles north of Oslo. It was founded in 1827. By the time of Nygaard's birth, the town had grown to a population of about four thousand people. The town itself is divided by a river that flows through its center and empties into the lake Mjösa. When not frozen over, the river was used by the lumbermen to float logs down to the sawmills, which were the town's principal industry. The district also had many small farms that dotted the surrounding country-side and its fertile valleys. The farmers brought their produce to the town for shipping across the lake and down to Oslo. The region possessed a very fine and healthy climate, and a number of sanatoria were built there for the care of people with res-piratory ailments. The landscape, too, was very beautiful, and because of this beauty certain famous Norwegian artists and writers had settled there. Nygaard's forebears had lived in this region for hundreds of years.

Nygaard's mother's maiden name was Emilie Johansen. She was a strikingly beautiful young woman who had been trained in medical midwifery. She had begun practicing in the community of Lillehammer when she married Johannes Nygaard, a mer-chant of the town. Their son Kaare Kristian was born to them on her twenty-fourth birthday in the year 1903. The birth went well for the mother and infant. Childbirth held no terror for this young woman who was schooled in the birth process.

Johannes Nygaard was a kindly man, and his son's first mem-ory of him was of his father patiently teaching him how to hold a spoon. Nygaard remembers also the sense of pride he felt that his father played the trumpet in the town band. The child mar-veled at this ability of his father's to make music. But Nygaard soon lost his gentle father, who died of sudden illness when the child was two and a half. Nygaard recalled that the death of his father left him more with a feeling of puzzlement than tragedy. His father lay inert and silent in death and could not summon the will to rise from the bed. In his child's mind, Nygaard thought: "If it were *me*, I would get up!" This tells us something about the resolution that even then was a marked attribute of Nygaard's character.

In psychoanalytic terms, the early loss of the father may not necessarily be a negative experience to the son. Often it is just the reverse, when the son is left the sole love object of an ador-ing mother. This was the case with Nygaard. His mother cherished

The English Barrister, bronze, 18 × 16 × 9
My Friend, the Village Idiot, 21 × 15 × 13, pp. 46, 47 (plaster of paris); pp. 48, 49 (bronze)
Father of the Village Idiot, bronze, 16 × 21 × 18, pp. 50 51
Lady with Large Hat, bronze, 17 × 5 × 5, pp. 52, 53
The Poet and Pegasus, bronze, 34 × 10 × 14, pp. 54, 55

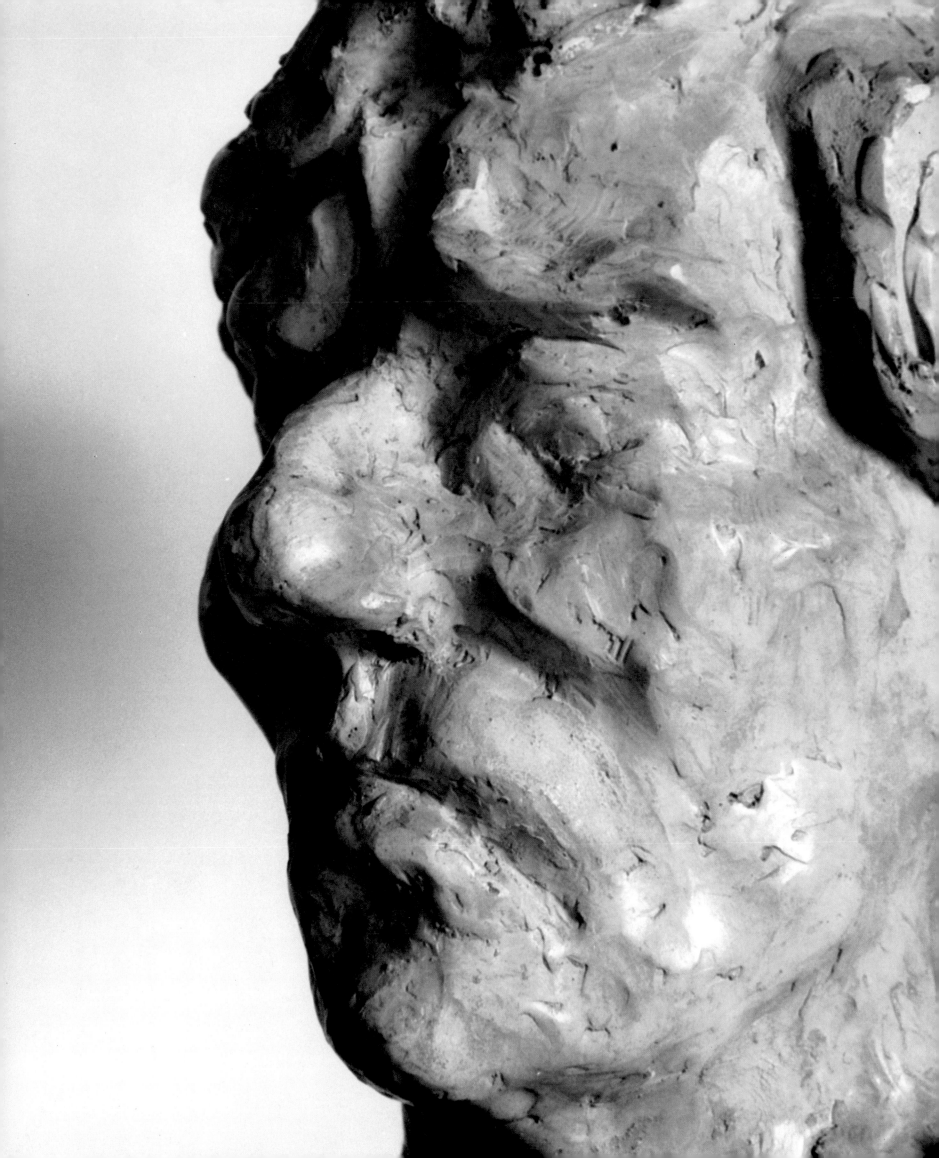

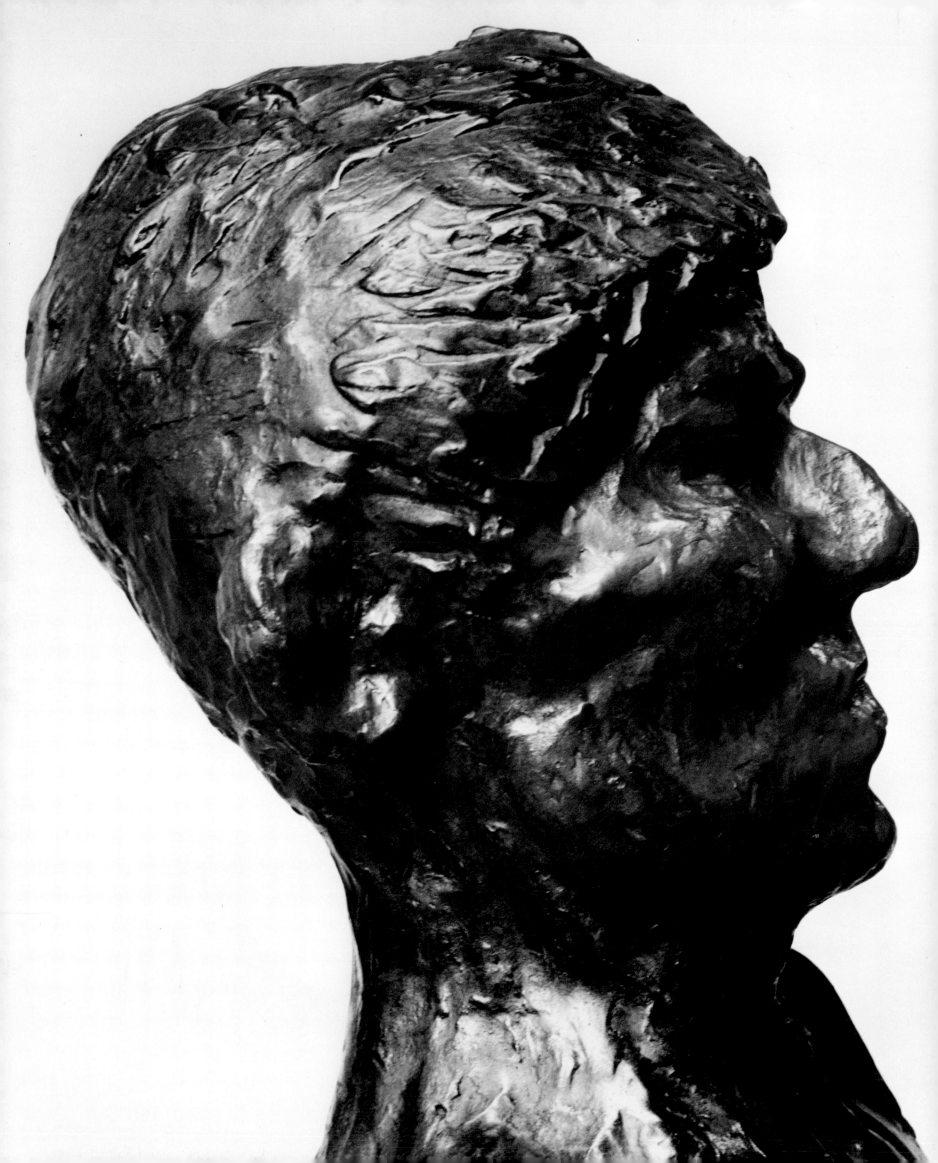

the boy, and he was also the delight of the maternal grandparents with whom they lived. It was a happy and vibrant home, too, filled with sturdy, energetic, and hardworking Norwegian souls.

The house was situated on the main street of the town on a large lot. There was a big family house in front, a smaller house in the middle of the property, and in the back there was a great yard where grandfather Johansen's blacksmith shop stood. This yard was always busy during the day. Nygaard recalls the great and powerful Norwegian Gubransdal horses that the local farmers led into the yard to be shod by grandfather Johansen and his assistant. And he remembers his grandmother's kitchen filled with the smell of fresh-baked bread and steaming pots of his favorite pea soup. The house was always full of life and, when on occasion his mother was called out at night to attend her patients in labor, the boy never felt alone, for the house seemed to breathe a sense of security and stability. But with the secure feeling, the small child also grew up with a mysterious sense of wonder because his own mother had a special knowledge that enabled her to help newborn life to come into the world!

From his mother's quiet and modest explanation of her work, the boy became aware early in life of the birth process and of the medical profession that helped life to live. She taught him about birth from her books on medical anatomy, which were stored in a special room with her articles on midwifery. So an early consciousness of medical service to life was instilled in him in a natural way. He grew with a sense of his own mother's thoughtful, vital work in a very human community, a community he could not fail to be aware of because it was all around him in so many ways.

There was the view from the front windows down to the river and lake with the rafts of logs coming down from the forests to the mills, and in the other direction beyond the town were the valleys and the towering mountains. The town itself teemed with activity. Across the street lived the town's first citizen, Dr. Torp, who was a family friend and advisor. Nearby was the lawyer Mr. Thallaug, who was the local representative to the Norwegian parliament, which is called the Storting. The dignified Mr. Bostad, too, was slightly awesome and forbidding because of his profession as an undertaker and casket manufacturer. Then there was jolly Mr. Helleberg, who made up for anyone else's solemnity with his friendly presence and his store full of sporting

Grazing Horse, bronze, 31 × 7½ × 20

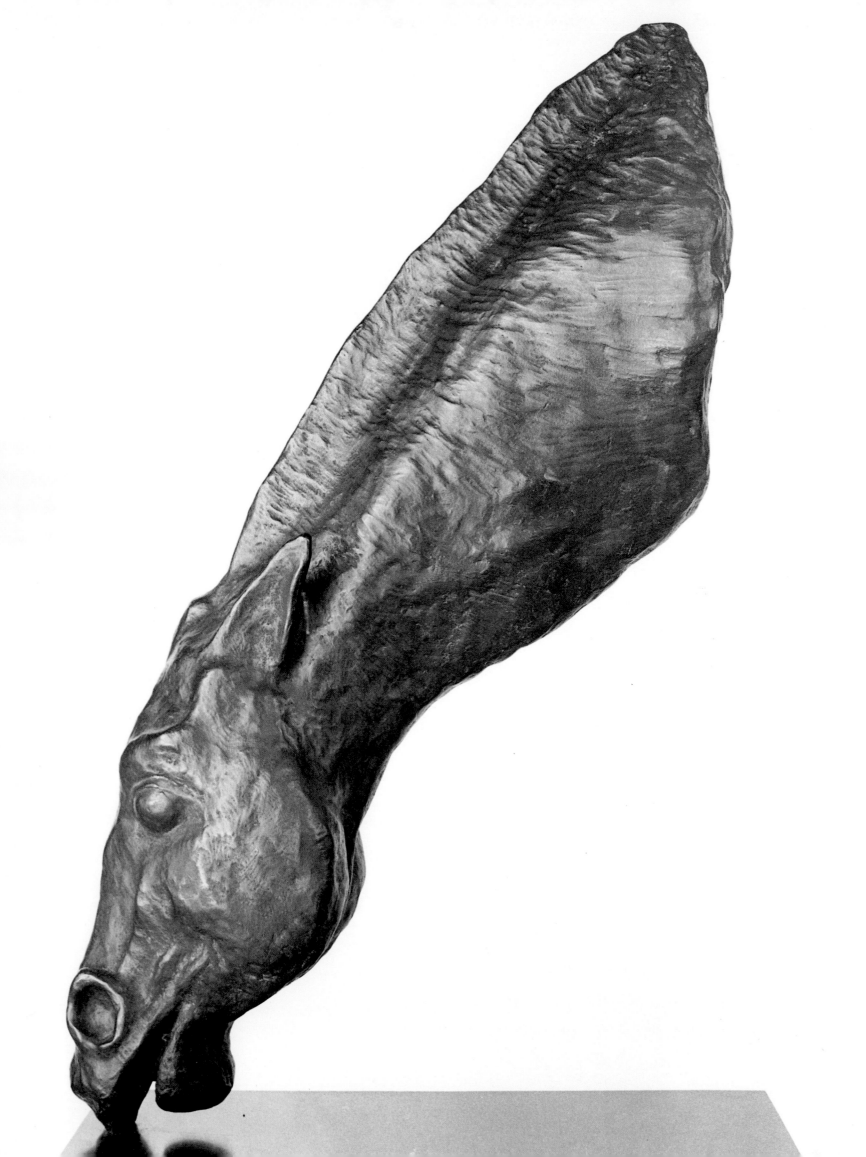

goods and all manner of things attractive to boys. All of these neighbors, to say nothing of the countrymen and farmers, knew the boy by name and greeted him as they brought their horses into the yard to the smithy. Nygaard was born into the midst of this lively community, and he felt himself to be a part of it all, the town, the land, and that vast thing beyond, yet always present, called Norway.

The boy's family was well off because they were hardworking, intelligent, and ethical people who had worked to create a modest and reasonable prosperity. During Nygaard's childhood and youth, the town of Lillehammer radiated this same prosperity, which was a product of hundreds of years of Norwegian vigor and honesty that grew from the soil itself. There were a few poor people in the town, a few wayward and luckless, as there are in any town. Overall there was a sure and sound sense that social justice was the way of life.

The town was bright, clean, and well built. Even on the other side of the river, where the factory and mill hands lived and where there were a few saloons (which gave rise to an occasional Saturday night fight), the houses had that neat and habitable quality and sense of underlying order that is typically Norwegian. But Nygaard had no sense of being humanly apart from the poor or the unfortunate, because his mother instilled in him her own sense of thoughtfulness and kindliness of soul for all people. Often when she went on calls, she took fresh-baked bread with her to give to the poorer women she cared for. So, with his sense of belonging, there grew a sense of caring for others.

Life for this bright and growing boy was rich in learning long before he started to go to school. The town was a part of his family life, and the people in it were his friends. As he grew, the countryside became a part of his life. He began to visit his paternal grandparents at their farm in a valley thirty miles away. When he went on boyish jaunts in the countryside, he met many of the famers who regularly brought their horses to be shod at the Johansen smithy. The valleys and the streams opened up for him. As he became aware of the world outside the town, he came to feel that he was a part of it, too.

An even larger world began for the boy when he became five and entered the *folkeskolen*. This new step began on a beautiful summer day in 1909. His mother put on her best dress and dressed him in the blue sailor suit that set off his own blond curls, which his mother was so fond of, and took him to school. Those curls soon became a subject of comment from his school-

Freedom Fighter up Against the Wall, fiberglass, 59 × 22 × 18
Viet Nam, bronze, 16 × 10 × 10, pp. 62, 63
Caveman, bronze, 12 × 10 × 11, pp. 64, 65
Concentration Camp Inmate—Hunger, bronze, 7½ × 4 × 4½, pp. 66, 67

mates, to his unhappiness, but he was a swifter runner than the other boys and he soon established his masculinity. His first great reward of education was a epidemic of head lice among the children, which served to rid him forever of the detested curls. Nygaard was enthusiastic about school from the beginning. His interest never flagged, and he went consistently on to great academic achievement.

The academic achievements are an important aspect of Nygaard's development, but now we must take into consideration the *two* main lines of development in Nygaard's life. One is the result of his academic strivings that led to his medical career. The other is the self-teaching creative forces that have operated quite independently in his life. These two lines of development have often run in independent and parallel directions in Nygaard's life, particularly during the course of his education. Only later, much later, were the two to come together. Because of these dual courses, and because medical science has been the strongest force in his life, we must first follow his academic development toward the medical profession. Later we will discuss the self-taught art process that emerged from his instincts to communicate his feelings.

The boy truly enjoyed school and drew from it all the benefits that good educators hope to give children. The first few years in the *folkeskolen* meant the enjoyment of competitive sports—running and soccer and wintertime skiing. It also meant learning to excell and compete in an exuberant way. He loved learning to write with a pen and ink . . . learning to write *words*! But learning was not confined to school. It increased at home, too.

A piano was purchased for the boy, and he began to study music with enthusiasm and pleasure. He continued to ponder over his mother's anatomy books, and he absorbed the atmosphere of the field of medicine from his mother and the family friend Dr. Torp. Most of all he loved to listen while his mother read to him in the evenings. She was particularly interested in history and read stories of famous men to him, implanting within him an affirmative image of masculine excellence. The bond between the mother and growing boy was very close: At times it seemed she was everything to him.

But instead of becoming overly dependent, the boy developed a strong sense of self-regulatory masculinity and independence. He grew aware of the possibility of overdependence on his mother one summer when he was staying with a friend in the

Fever, bronze, 6 × 7½ × 5

country. He was allowed to use the telephone to call home everyday and speak to his mother. His friend's family playfully teased him about his eagerness to make these calls. This made him realize his calls home were preventing him from enjoying his experiences with his friends to the fullest extent and were, in a sense, depriving them of his full participation. So he took himself in hand and learned to regulate his feelings to situations and people. This was a very useful lesson for a future physician, and a lesson that was to soon prove of importance in his family life.

In 1913, when Nygaard was nine, his mother married a merchant of Lillehammer named Nils Simensen. This was in some respects a blow to the boy, who had held the first place in his mother's affections until then, and he did not quite know how to cope with it. Though his new stepfather was an extremely kind man, the boy knew that the special closeness he had had with his mother was broken and that it would never be the same again. He instinctively knew he should turn his feelings toward the world, and though he became a bit more inward, he also became stronger in his sense of resolution, more committed to his schoolwork.

The sense of loss lingered for some time, but it was softened the following year when he entered the middle school. With this change came a new awareness of the beauty of girls, Norwegian girls who were so vibrant and womanly, girls who were so physically active and such good skiers! It was a new time of boys and girls together at skiing, swimming, and tramping through the countryside. How the shy and reserved boy loved those times.

The schoolmaster of the middle school helped Nygaard find other, more academic, forms of love as well. This man managed to transmit his own great love of literature to his students. The youth awakened under his guidance to the love of language: Goethe and Schiller and the great Norwegian writers Ibsen, Björnson, and Wergeland. This schoolmaster was remarkable for his ability to instill in students a real respect for these men of letters, and this was a wonderful period of intellectual expansion for Nygaard. Other kinds of understanding emerged at this time as well: Nygaard felt a new sense of the importance of Norwegian freedom and liberty. World War I had started and German submarines had begun to attack Norwegian shipping. This touched all Norwegians because the Norwegian maritime tradition had always been a major aspect of the country's life. His new awareness of Norway's great cultural heritage and the war's

The Art Critic, bronze, 14 × 8 × 13
The Museum Director, bronze, 20 × 25 × 16, pp. 72, 73

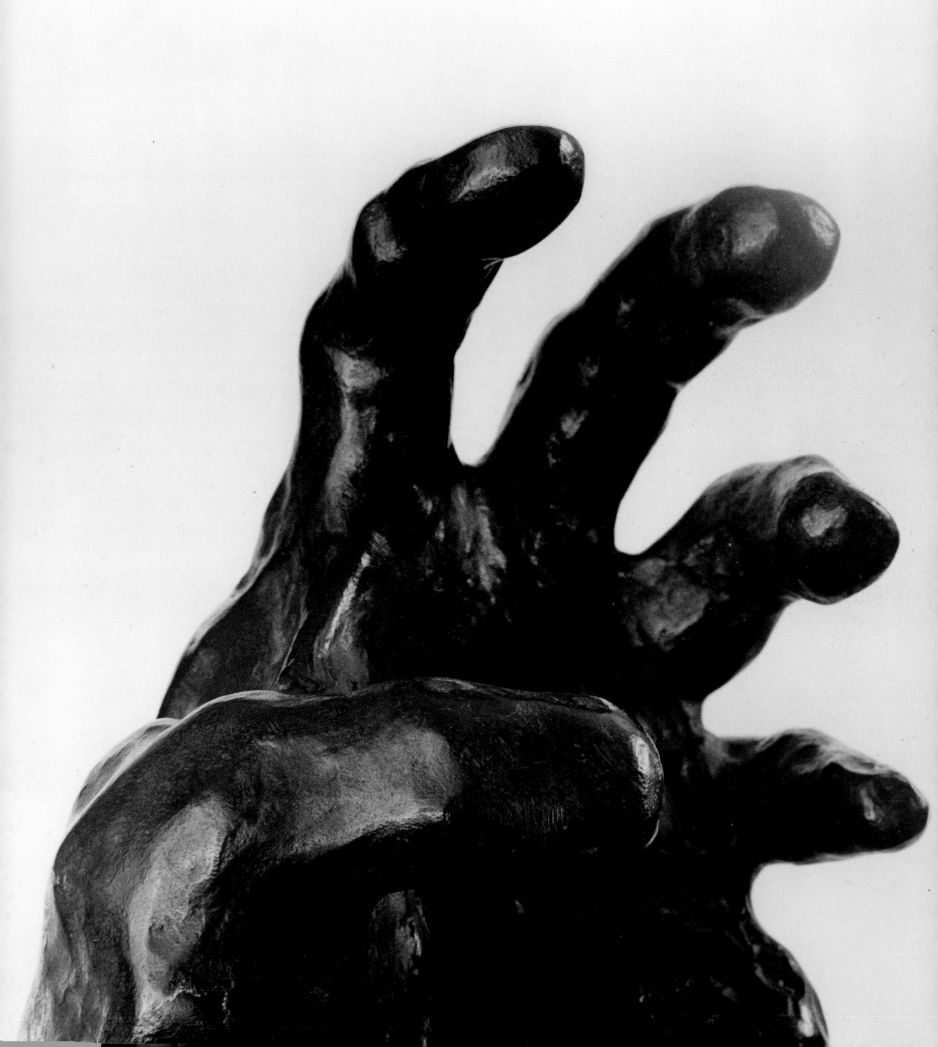

challenge to the country's freedom gave the youth stronger feelings of his identity. Then as the war progressed, two powerful events occurred that impressed Nygaard forever.

The first of these events resulted from the German torpedoing of the British cruiser India off the Norwegian coast in 1916. Eight hundred men of the British crew survived the attack and were taken into custody by the Norwegian government. They were transported to Lillehammer, where they were interned for the remainder of the war. The entry of these sailors into Lillehammer was the first large influx of foreigners in the town. To Nygaard and the other boys, these men were heroes who far surpassed those of the imagination or those read about in books. This experience also set more profound thoughts in motion in Nygaard's consciousness; he began to puzzle the question about why men went to war in the first place. This question became more serious to him when he became acquainted with some of the men. The commander, Captain Kennedy, married a Norwegian woman whose baby was delivered by Nygaard's mother. He began to meditate on the human side of heroism, and his awareness of human complexity and tragedy became far more real than a literary experience. Shortly after this event, another occurred that deepened Nygaard's insights further.

The Russian Revolution of 1917 set in motion events that were to have a lasting effect on this young man. The revolution had cataclysmic effects on the Russian people; countless thousands were uprooted and had to flee for their lives. These émigrés streamed across European and Asiatic borders carrying what few clothes, possessions, and valuables they could salvage from the chaos. Some of them reached Lillehammer and were given shelter there, by being billeted in various homes. Five of these refugees were taken into the Johansen-Simensen household, where Nygaard came to know them well.

Four of these refugees were members of a Russian family of some means: the mother, two daughters—one about thirty, another of about eighteen—and a son of fifteen. They were members of a once large and prosperous Russian family. They had managed to bring a few gemstones (possibly diamonds) with them, secreted in the linings of their clothes. These were converted into cash enough to pay for sustenance for a while. Once their money was gone, the women, being untrained, were unable to work, and only the son found employment as a factory hand. Nygaard felt the uprooted bewilderment in this shattered family; their sense of heartbreak and loss permeated the middle

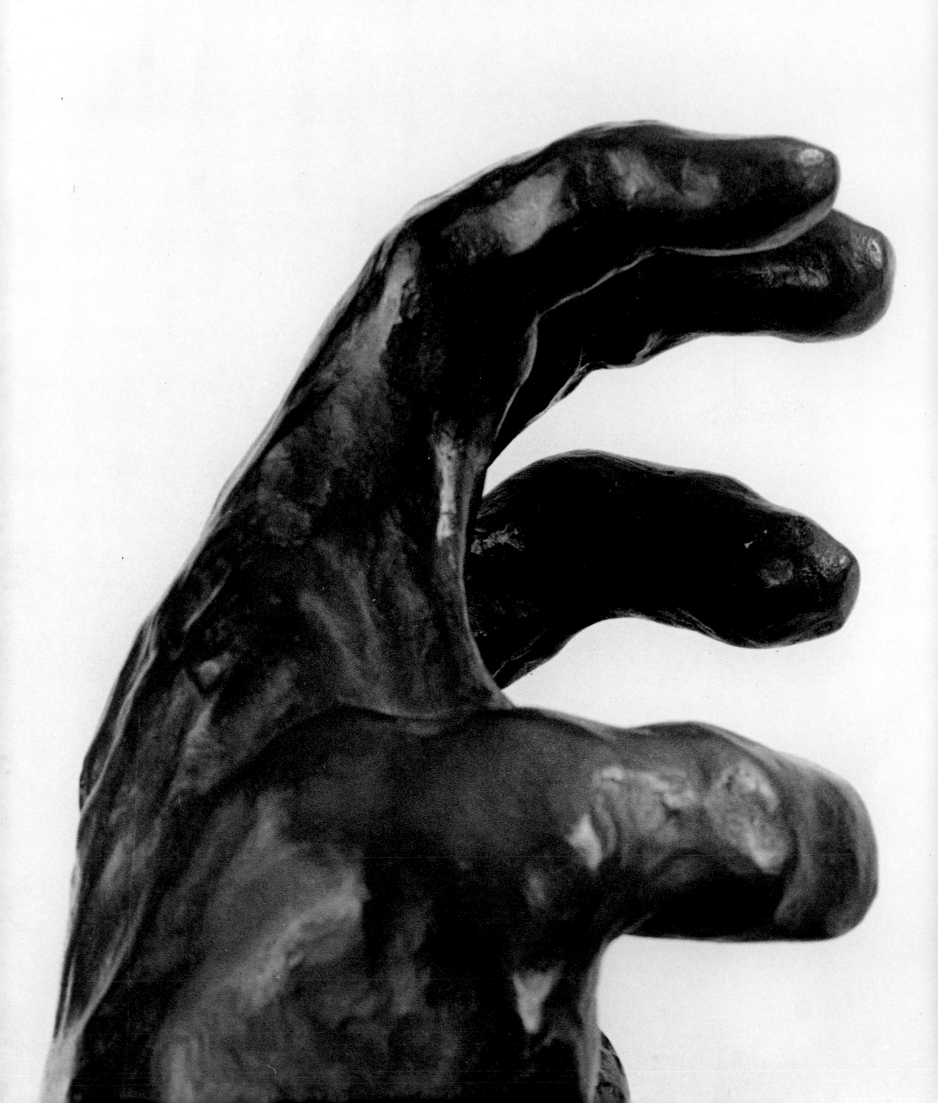

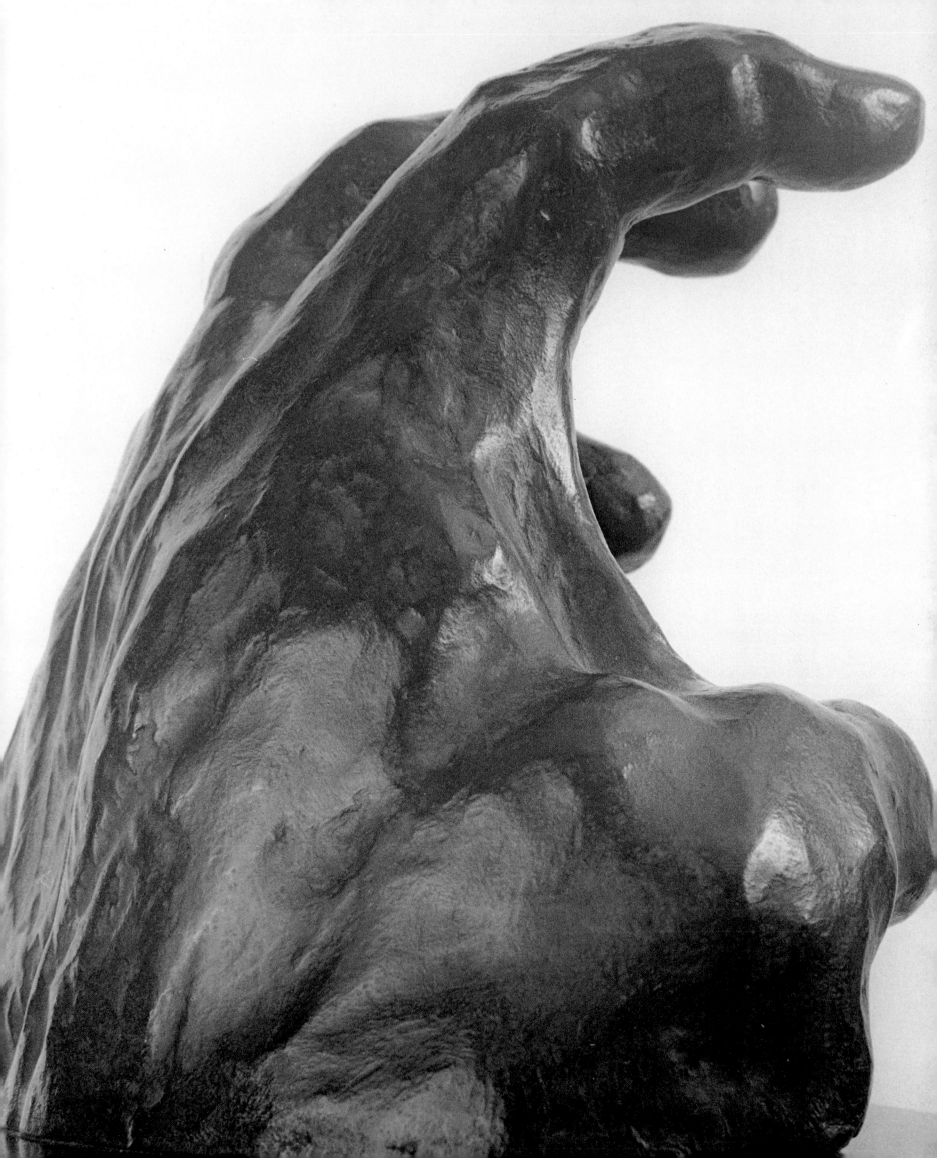

Exodus, bronze, 4½ × 12 × 6½

house next to the blacksmith's shop, which had been given to the Russians to live in while they remained in Lillehammer.

A fifth refugee also lived in the middle house, in a loft in the attic, which had been Nygaard's own domain. This was an elderly and dignified lawyer. This man was a gentleman of considerable learning, and he took a genuine interest in young Nygaard. The two got on well together. A friendship developed between them that revolved around literary interests. From this gentleman, Nygaard first learned of the writings of Dostoevski, a writer in whom he has retained a lifelong interest. There was something Dostoevskian in the old man himself that aroused in Nygaard a sense of both faith and tragedy. The old gentleman, hard up for funds and fighting to survive, purchased a portable electric saw and attempted to earn his livelihood by going from house to house offering to cut firewood. He was not successful in this venture, being old, a foreigner, and not suited to manual labor, but to Nygaard it was a lesson in the fragile nature of human dignity. The plight of all these people touched Nygaard's heart deeply. The lessons he learned from these fragile souls perhaps helped him make the decision he was soon to make on his career.

In 1918, the year the war ended, Nygaard entered the *gymnasium* looking forward to the three years of intensive study and preparation to meet the qualifications for entry into the university. Entering the gymnasium meant that he would soon have to decide what his career would be. He was still somewhat shy and reserved, still active and competitive in sports, still an intense and serious student. He had considerable ability and talent in several areas, but he faced the formidable responsibility of consciously having to choose his life's work. This is not always an easy task for young people when they have several talents. He had a serious problem in making this decision because his great love for music was balanced by his interest in medicine.

Over the years, his love of music had grown and his musicianship had advanced to the point where he seriously considered becoming a concert pianist. On the other hand, he had grown up in an atmosphere where medical service and the sense of human responsibility were always present. If anything, the experience of the war had emphasized the importance of service to mankind. This conflict occupied his thoughts for almost a year. In 1919, during his second year at the gymnasium, with strong encouragement from his mother he decided to enter medicine. This was a field he had been familiar with from his earliest days

and one for which he was extremely well suited by ability and temperament. The correctness of his choice was borne out by the fact that he was to pursue this field with determination and wisdom for close to fifty years. He began strongly: On only rare occasions would a student of the gymnasium finish the three-year course receiving the highest qualifications for entrance to the university . . . Nygaard was one of those.

When Nygaard entered the University of Oslo Medical School in 1922, he left behind the warm family and community of Lillehammer. It was an abrupt break with all the supportive family warmth, the friendships, and familiar surroundings that had nourished a happy childhood and youth. But he carried with him the qualities his background had bred into him: warmth of character, honesty, loyalty, and faith. Oslo was a city that was not easy for students then, and not always warm, kindly, or accepting. Nygaard lived alone for the first time in his life in a series of small rooms that had none of the warmth of the house in Lillehammer which had breathed such life. But he was equal to the tasks of life and soon found out that what Oslo lacked in personal warmth it made up for with the National Museum, the theater, and concerts. Nygaard settled into the routine of his medical studies with diligence, patience, and calm judgment. And it is not surprising that he completed his medical studies in 1929 and graduated cum laude. He had been well nurtured and was now able to cope with life's problems. People felt that great things would come from young Dr. Nygaard.

Aside from the gradual accumulation of medical knowledge during this period, the single most important occurrence during the Oslo years was his meeting with a young physiotherapist named Ella Frey in 1927. Ella was a lovely young woman of very good family. She lived in Oslo with her mother, older brother, and younger sister. The Freys were a wealthy landowning family that had possessed vast tracts of farmland and forest north of Oslo for several hundred years. In the financial panic of 1898, the family lost the estate that had been in their possession for generations. Shortly thereafter, they moved to Oslo to begin the renewal of their fortunes. The beautiful and patrician Ella was also industrious and self-confident, and it is again not surprising the two were drawn to one another. Nygaard became engaged to Ella in 1928.

Though the year 1929 was the beginning of an international depression, it was the start of a hopeful twelve-year period of study and hard work for Nygaard, whose industry and drive

In the Sweat of Your Brow Shall You Earn Your Bread, bronze, 21 × 11½ × 17, pp. 82, 84, 85
Pietà, bronze, 9 × 7½ × 14, pp. 86, 87, 88

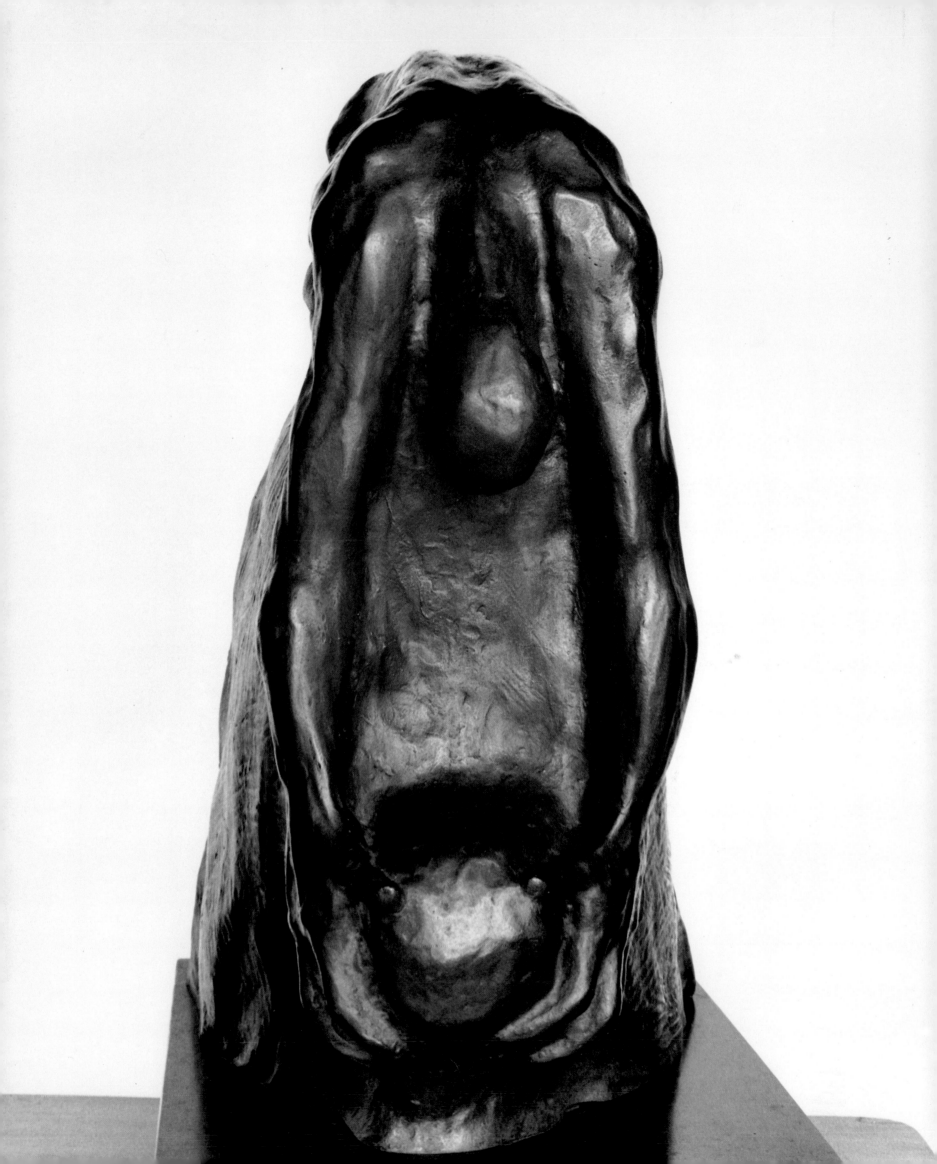

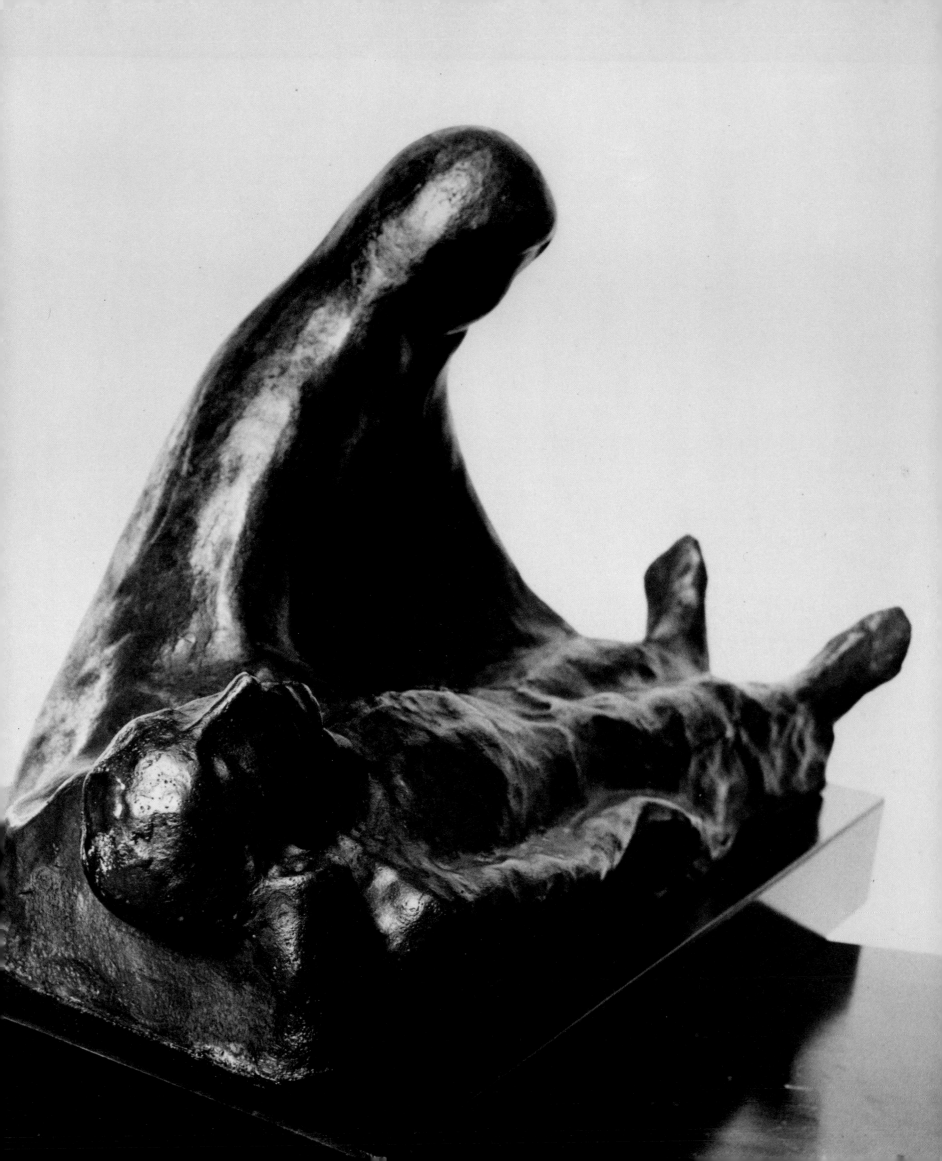

never faltered with the bad times. This was the beginning of his study in his specialization and his medical research that was to involve several major changes of habitat. Right after leaving medical school, Nygaard worked as a general practitioner in a small country town for six months, until May of 1930, when he sailed to the United States to accept a general assistantship in surgery at the Gundersen Clinic at LaCrosse, Wisconsin. To some, the sudden change to a new country and new ways might have required a long period of adjustment, but Nygaard felt no such difficulties and adapted quickly to his work in surgery. He began to do research on spinal anesthesia, comparing its effects to those of general anesthesia (a study that was later published in 1935 in a Scandinavian scientific journal).

This study of the effects of spinal anesthesia had very fortunate results in another respect. The young Dr. Nygaard submitted it in his application for an assistantship at the Mayo Clinic, and it caught the attention of the director of the Mayo Foundation. This led to Nygaard's being accepted at the Mayo Clinic as fellow in surgery in 1931. This was truly a wonderful opportunity for the young surgeon from Norway, as it enabled him to study with two masters of surgery: Drs. Will and Charley Mayo. Nygaard responded to this opportunity with his characteristic zeal and resolution to excell. His determined effort was rewarded when he was chosen as the first assistant in surgery to the Mayo brothers and later to the surgeon who succeeded them, Dr. Waltman Walters.

The engagement to Ella Frey continued happily. She joined him in the United States, where they were married in Chicago in 1933. The Chicago World's Fair was a great attraction at that time, and the young couple toured it on their honeymoon. They then returned to Rochester and the Mayo Clinic, and Nygaard continued as first assistant. In 1937 he was appointed assistant professor of surgery at Oslo University. This brought the Nygaards back to Oslo, where they were to remain until 1940.

This university professorship was another situation that had two-fold advantages for Nygaard. In addition to allowing him to teach, it afforded him unique opportunities to continue the research project he had been engaged in for several years. During his time at the Mayo Clinic, he had started independent research on the coagulation of the blood in relation to surgical problems. This work was done during his free time, in addition to his work in surgery. Nygaard continued this research in Oslo with special reference to the problems of bleeding in newborn

infants. The research opportunities that were part of the advantages of his affiliation with the university allowed him to carry his work forward with great success. He soon developed a technique for measuring coagulability of blood with an instrument of his own invention that utilized the photo-electric cell. This instrument was called the photelgraph, and it is the same essential method that is being used to measure blood coagulability at the present time. When this research came to its final stages prior to publication in 1940, the Nygaards left Oslo to come to the United States so Nygaard could do the final stages of technical research for his project in the library of the New York Academy of Medicine. They arrived in January of 1940.

After several months of work, this final technical research was completed in New York. Nygaard was then given the position of research assistant by the directors of Mayo Clinic—who were very interested in his work—while he was finishing the final draft of the book for the publisher. It was published under the title *Hemorrhagic Diseases: Photo-electric Study of Blood Coagulability*, St. Louis, C. V. Mosby Company, 1941. This book was the culmination of a rich twelve-year period of intensive work during which time Nygaard had devoted himself to the mastery of abdominal surgery under the Mayo brothers and had successfully conducted his own independent research projects. As the era of the 1930s closed with such significant accomplishments for Nygaard, another era was to open for him, which would make further and greater demands on his abilities and stamina.

Nygaard had planned to settle into a quiet professional life after the publication of his book. He had applied for a license to practice in New York State, because he had been offered a position of associate in surgery at White Plains Hospital in Westchester County. When he was granted the New York license, Nygaard accepted this position, and the young couple moved to White Plains. In certain respects the couple's dream of stability came true, for Nygaard remained with this hospital for the rest of his career as a surgeon—a period of over thirty-five years. With this new position, an unsuspected flood of work and responsibility came that was far larger than Nygaard had ever imagined.

On the night of April 9, 1940, Norway was invaded by the German army. C. J. Hambro, the great Norwegian statesman, was able to arrange the evacuation of the king, the royal household, the cabinet, and many of the members of the Storting shortly before the Germans arrived in Oslo. The Norwegian gov-

The Borgia Pope, bronze, 14 × 21 × 17½

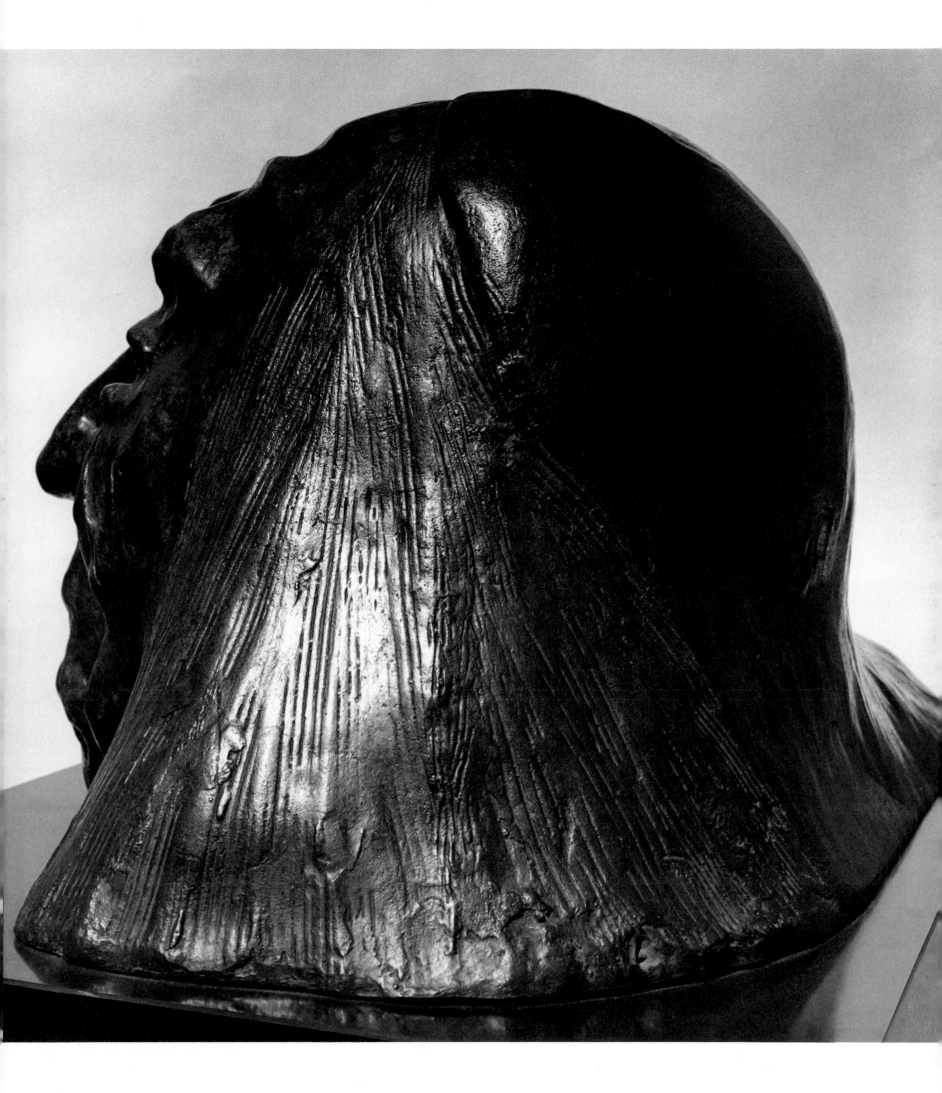

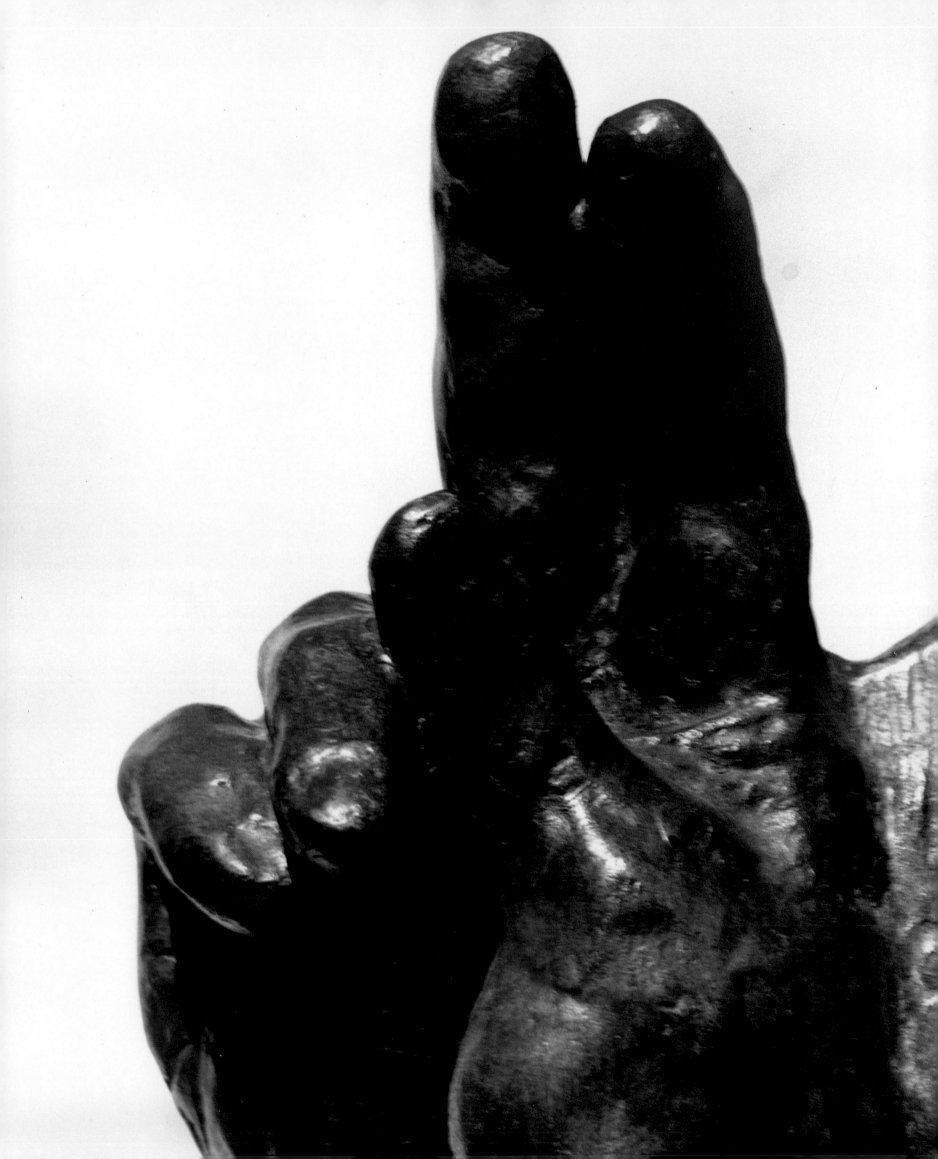

ernment immediately ordered all Norwegian ships to neutral ports. Some 1,100 ships were thereby kept out of German hands and ordered to proceed to the United States and take part in the war on the side of the Allies. The Norwegian government organized them into a shipping concern that did wartime duty in the North Atlantic.

Shipping in the North Atlantic during World War II was one of the most hazardous tasks of the war because the ships were under constant threat of attack by the German submarine fleet. Conscious of this continuing threat to the seamen, the Norwegian government in exile organized a health service in New York City to serve Norwegian seamen. Nygaard immediately offered his services to this organization. Acting on his own initiative, he promptly went to the board of directors of the White Plains Hospital with a plan to set up an emergency hospital service for the Norwegian seamen. The board responded by giving facilities for thirty-five beds. Nygaard directed this emergency medical facility for the injured seamen for the next five years. During this period, four thousand wartime casualties were taken care of until the service was discontinued shortly after the war's end.

Nygaard's wartime duties often involved as many as fifteen surgery cases a day in addition to cases coming from his small private practice. He also visited up to fifty postoperative and ambulatory cases everyday. His cases ran the gamut from injuries caused by shelling, burn cases, and standard shipboard accidents to seamen found suffering from exposure in lifeboats. The year 1942 was the worst. Submarines were lying in wait for the merchant ships just outside of New York harbor. Convoys left on Fridays, and quite often Nygaard had to find men to help crew the ships from among his ambulatory patients. His responsibilities were of the gravest kind, but he ran the whole facility working often as long as eighteen hours a day, never letting down in his own devotion to duty.

In recognition of his wartime service, Nygaard was awarded the Order of St. Olaf, Knight First Class, by the king of Norway in 1948. This order, one of the most highly respected orders of honor in the world, was given in recognition of Nygaard's dedicated and faithful service to Norway.

Throughout his wartime services, Nygaard continued to serve medicine by writing articles on various scientifically interesting aspects of his surgical cases. This gives us some idea of his

The Musician, bronze, 9½ × 5 × 4½
Homage to Paul Gauguin, bronze, 9 × 6 × 5½, pp. 98, 99, 101

dedication, and it also demonstrates his ability to concentrate and to function under enormous burdens of work. We must take this into consideration when we discuss later his ability to produce sculpture while carrying on a full-time medical career. It is also not surprising that this great capacity for work led to a large growth in his private practice once his wartime duties were finished. This did not happen through connections or social contacts but solely through his reputation for excellence in surgery.

Things improved for the Nygaards financially, but they continued to live a modest and simple life. Their first home in White Plains was an apartment, which they lived in until 1946. They then purchased their own home, where they lived comfortably until 1958, at which time they moved to the present house in which Nygaard still lives. They were quiet and happy in their home life. Their interests revolved around Nygaard's medical work, concerts, lectures, and art exhibits, and from time to time they would entertain friends for dinner. These friends were an unusually interesting and distinguished group of people.

Trygve Lie was secretary general of the United Nations during these years, and Nygaard was both friend and personal physician to this most distinguished Norwegian. Through this close friendship, Nygaard was brought into contact with behind-the-scenes views of the world events of those days that were to make lasting impressions upon him. For example, one Sunday morning Nygaard was called to attend Trygve Lie. The secretary general of the United Nations had been up all the previous night negotiating and trying to prevent the outbreak of the Korean War, which had thundered into history that very morning. Nygaard recalls that Lie had said to him: "Of all these people, I seem to be the only one who really knows how it is possible for a country and its people to lose their liberty overnight." To Nygaard, it was as though his own fingers were touching not just the pulse of one man, but the pulse of an ailing and troubled world.

Another close friend of this same period was the aforementioned C. J. Hambro. Hambro was a Norwegian statesman of truly international stature. He had been the last president of the first great organization attempting to establish international peace—the League of Nations—and he played a major role in establishing the Norwegian government in exile during World War II. C. J. Hambro was the Norwegian representative to the United Nations during the late 1940s, and it was at this period that the friendship between the two men deepened into a lasting one. For Nygaard there was a poignant sense of sorrow knowing

Homage to Paul Gauguin
Vincent Van Gogh, bronze, 19 × 4½ × 6, pp. 102, 103
Homage to Vincent Van Gogh, bronze, 20½ × 6 × 5½, pp. 104, 105

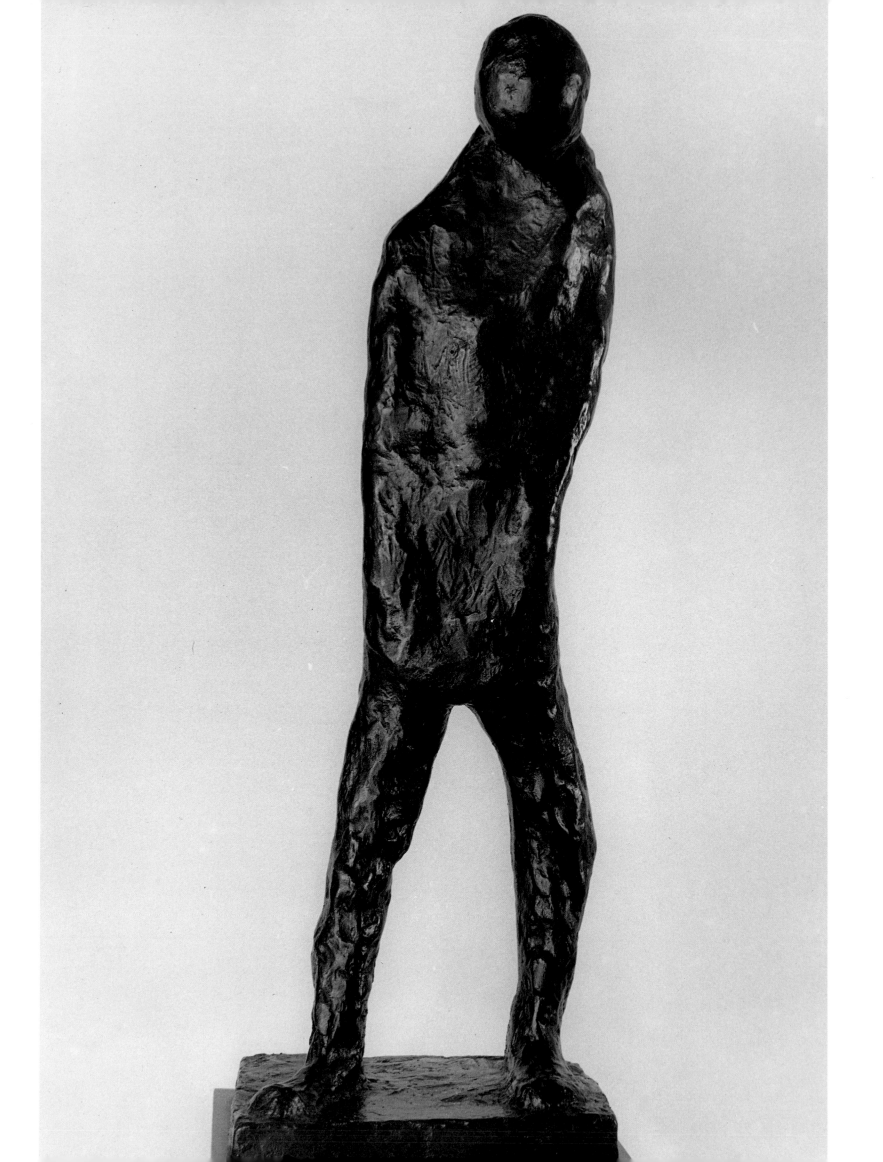

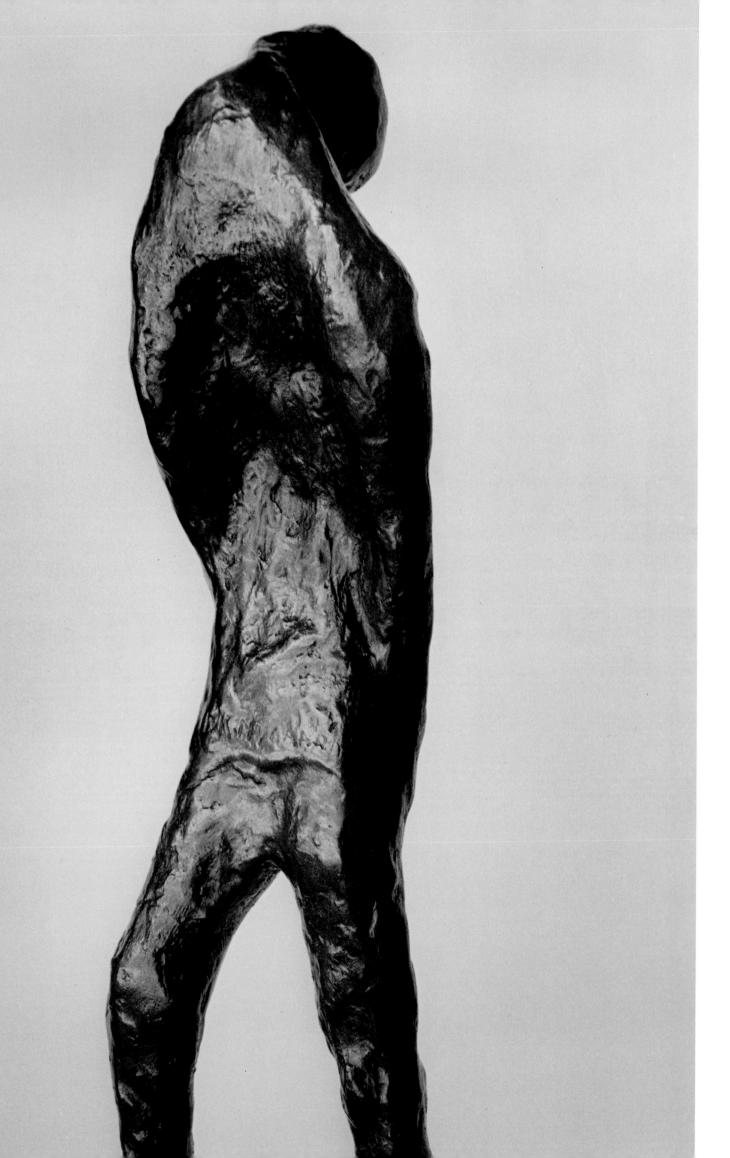

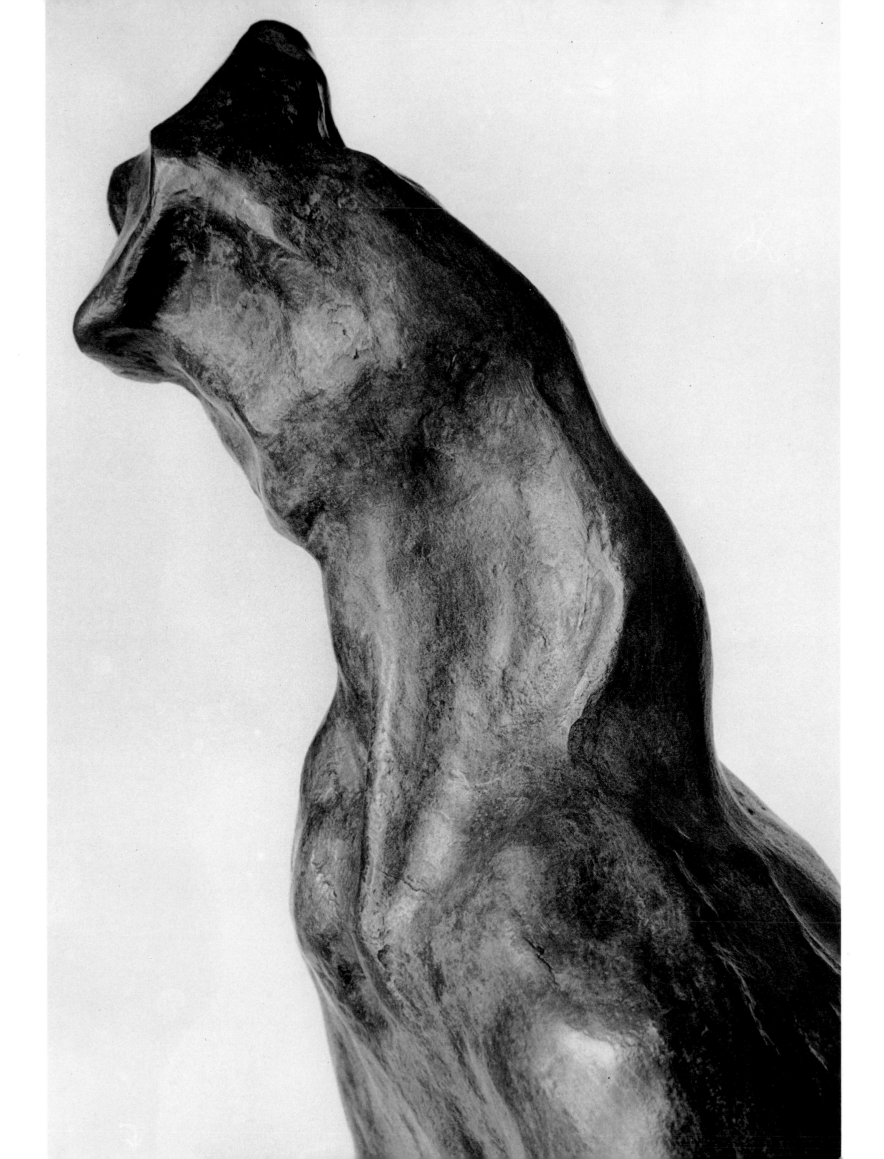

men of such great ability, who had tried to establish rationality in this world, and who had lived through exile and defeat of their goals, though not their spirits. Through these two distinguished and intimate friends, he felt he also administered to the anguished hopes of the twentieth century, a century that has stepped from one disaster to another. In spite of the current of international events, Nygaard's own hopeful spirits continued to expand.

Though his practice continued to grow and flourish during the postwar years, he was still aiming toward another goal of public responsibility. For many years, he had planned to apply for the chair of the professor of surgery at the University of Oslo when the position became vacant. This was Nygaard's ultimate gesture of responsibility toward his native Norway, and for years he had studied with his goal in mind. . . . He felt a moral obligation to Norwegian medicine to compete for this position. As it turned out, the competition was narrowed down to Nygaard and another man, and the other man was chosen for the post. Much to his own surprise, Nygaard was quite relieved that he was not chosen. Something quite new to him began to open up: After many years of completely dedicated service and study . . . personal freedom!

This freedom was more of the spirit than anything else because Nygaard continued in his strenuous pattern of medical work. The liberation he felt was release from his most serious obligations to the past. His present obligations to his profession continued along with the twelve-hour working day that began at six in the morning, with an afternoon break, and resumed until around ten at night. With an expanding practice, Nygaard took another surgeon into partnership and later on took several highly accomplished young assistants as his own reputation in surgery grew. For the remainder of his career in medicine, Nygaard's freedom was only of that inner sort, that of a man who has mastered an extremely difficult profession and who functions in it with complete personal responsibility.

It is from this position of high professional responsibility and total dedication to his work in surgery that we will now consider Nygaard as an artist. Because it was only after having achieved this position that he felt the inner need and freedom to express the things in art that were welling up from his experience and feelings.

Now that we have examined the principal features of Nygaard's education and his career in surgery, we can study the

Rodin, bronze, 24 × 21 × 16

development of his work in sculpture. We can now trace the forces in his life that led to the emergence of his creative impulses. We will follow the hidden lines of the completely different inner development that took place from the beginning of his life on through the strenuous years of his medical training, his apprenticeship at the Mayo Clinic, and the wartime service, which led to his final mastery of his profession. What were these subsurface streams that gathered force and began to emerge in 1951? To find them we must go back again to his earliest years.

Art was in the very air that Nygaard breathed from his earliest years. His home was no stranger to art, paper and pencils were at hand from the beginning, and the boy soon discovered the pleasure of drawing the people, dogs, and horses that were always present in the big backyard. As soon as he was old enough, he joined the children of the neighborhood in their enthusiasm for collecting and exchanging the popular penny picture cards that were then sold in the local stationery store. (His favorite was a fierce watchdog with a heroic expression.) There was art of a more serious kind in the classical Apollo cast in plaster that belonged to his mother, which the boy contemplated with growing curiosity. In the local park, a block away from his home, there was a chaste bronze figure of Leda and a somewhat conservative swan placed in the center of the small lake. The boy felt this Leda was the most beautiful thing in the world. Near his father's grave in the local churchyard were other sculptures, ones of bereavement and death: angels, figures of women meditating, sorrowing mother and child figures, which were a part of everyone's experience then because of the high infant mortality rates of those times. The serious boy observed all of these things with an honest and uncynical gravity, and he understood the respectful and serious intent behind them.

There was something else that was even more personally meaningful to the young boy than all of these local examples of art, and this was the ornamental ironwork done for the town's most important building by his grandfather Johansen. His own grandfather's decorative iron balustrade circled the gallery of the grand ballroom of the town hall. In addition, his grandfather's beautiful ironwork decorated the steeple of the same building! A personal and public statement of art by a member of his family and his own mother's gentle watercolor painting put the boy in touch with the idea that art was something accessible and within his reach and that it emerged from human strength

Percy Grainger, Pianist, Composer, Musical Genius, plaster of paris for bronze, 9 × 16 × 8   109

and human tenderness. Whatever his instinctive responses were we cannot ever know, but the seeds of art began to germinate within his own being, and his experiences in school affected their growth.

When Nygaard first entered the *folkeskolen*, a piece of sculpture that hung in the hallway was one of the first things that caught his attention and held it. This happened to be a plaster cast of a head of Björnson done by the great Norwegian sculptor Gustav Vigeland. It was a powerful head with strong and commanding features, and the boy meditated on this as he had on his mother's cast of Apollo. There were, in addition, pictures of pieces of classical sculpture and architecture that hung in the classrooms, and one of these turned out to be that bit of classical rhubarb that has given many a schoolboy the jimjams down through the ages . . . the Laocoön. Nygaard was shaken by that work because he felt Laocoön was losing the battle with the snake even though he had the muscular development that should have enabled him to win. To Nygaard, this seemed unreasonable, but perhaps gave him the insight that heroism and muscular development do not necessarily go hand in hand. In addition to these meditative stimulations provided by the *folkeskolen*, there were drawing classes that were given daily dealing with the more practical aspects of drawing shapes.

In the community itself, there was another very rich source of art experience: the popular Museum of Norwegian Folk Art and Craft that had been put up through the efforts of a local dentist, Mr. Anders Sandvig, who was devoted to preserving the great heritage of the art and craft of the region. The examples that this devoted man had personally collected and housed in the museum went as far back as the ninth century. There were all sorts of folk paintings and carvings, objects of everyday utility, and buildings used for every purpose in former times. Nygaard loved this place and visited it often, and this experience was quite important to his artistic development. It gave him a living example of his own Norwegian heritage in art, a heritage that went back for hundreds of years!

From the *folkeskolen* Nygaard graduated to the middle school, which was not far from his own house. When this school was opened in 1864, Henrik Ibsen wrote a poem in honor of the event. Ibsen's interest coupled with the personal enthusiasm for Norwegian literature expressed by the school's director gave Nygaard a sense that the middle school had a direct connection to Norwegian art. The curriculum included classes in drawing, in

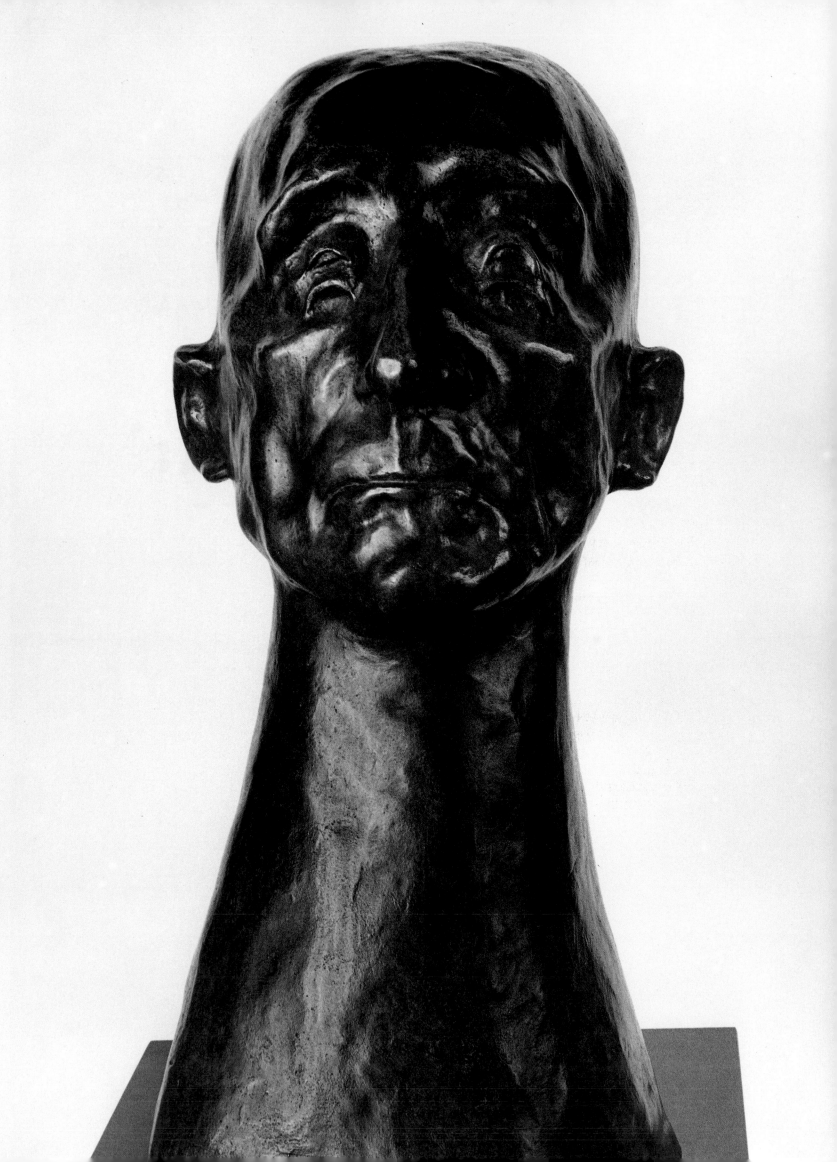

which there was a great deal of freedom. The drawing classes given each day were often held in the open, and they involved drawing from nature and drawing from everyday experience. They were given by a teacher who was herself an artist.

At this period in his life, Nygaard became fully aware of the practicing artists who lived in Lillehammer and its environs. Among these was the writer Sigrid Undset, who was to win the Nobel Prize for literature in 1928. There was the lyric painter Thorvald Erichsen, who had studied painting in Paris with Matisse. There was Lars Jorde, a robust and joyful landscape painter. There was the sculptor Rolf Lunde, whose bronze figures were done in the Rodin tradition. And all their studios were hospitably open to those interested in their work, a fact that young Nygaard soon learned to value. He first visited their studios to marvel, and then began to yearn toward art himself. Then something quite unusual and unexplainable began to happen to the young man. . . . He experienced a sudden outpouring of creativity.

Taking into consideration Nygaard's rich home life, his awareness of his native heritage in art, and the art life in the community, it is not surprising that he felt the pull of the forces of art within himself. He began to respond independently to them as he started to mature into manhood. This sudden surge of creative impulse occurred when he was fifteen years old. He made his first serious independent attempts to paint and make sculpture. He made the sculpture in direct plaster. They were heads done from imagination. He also attempted a portrait of his grandfather done from life. In painting he did an imaginary young girl sitting in a garden chair, then a portrait of his grandmother done from life, and several landscapes. But his most interesting work—in view of later developments—was a painting he did of his own interpretation of Moses viewing the Promised Land. This subject indicated an early interest in the symbolic representation of the relationship between lawfulness and the human impulse for gratification. This concern was quite appropriate for a boy who was undergoing the transition to manhood, a boy who seemed to have a natural ability for sustained work and emotional self-regulation.

This sudden release of artistic creativity lasted only a few brief months. Young Nygaard was preparing to enter the gymnasium. He was embarking on years of intensive study that would continue without letup until 1950. Not till that thirty-year period came to a close would he have the time or opportunity for artistic creativity again. His interest in painting and sculpture was to

continue during the intervening years; his inner yearnings toward art were nourished by visits to museums whenever possible and by the gradual accumulation of books on art. In Oslo, during his medical training and professorship at the university, Nygaard lived in the presence of two great Norwegian geniuses. Both the painter Edvard Munch and the sculptor Gustav Vigeland radiated a sense of their presence to all Norwegians. Nygaard was particularly interested by both of them. He caught glimpses of the aging Munch at the university, and several times he went out to Frogner Park to peer through the fence at the work in progress at the studio of the reclusive Vigeland. That was very heady air to breathe for a young man with his artistic fires banked!

Nygaard's visit to the Chicago World's Fair was an especially stimulating art experience for the young surgeon in 1933. There were large exhibitions of the work of Rodin, Malvina Hoffman, and Ivan Meštrović. Then a few years later, once the Nygaards had settled in White Plains, there were the New York museums: the Metropolitan, the Frick, and the Museum of Modern Art. All of these things were seen by Nygaard in the precious free time that was available to the busy surgeon. These experiences helped to build the great creative impetus in him that was finally to break forth again in 1951.

When the responsibility toward the Oslo University professorship in surgery was behind him, Nygaard experienced a large sense of release. He found himself in a situation of personal freedom he had not experienced since 1918. He was happily married to Ella, earning a substantial income. His life was comfortable and serene, and for the first time in many years he had the open possibilities of free time. Not very much free time, it was true. That small amount existed within the confines of his full-time surgical practice. Nevertheless there existed certain possibilities for Nygaard to let his imagination and fancy run free.

Knowing something of Nygaard's ability to sustain work over long periods of time, we can understand that he *needed* some outlet for his abundant energies. With his capacity for work, it is not surprising that he turned to art for release. . . . It had always been there waiting, part of him needing fulfillment.

He began by painting, making copies of masterworks done by his favorite painters, for example, Munch and Gauguin. Then he went on to work from nature. He soon discovered that there was

Joseph Hirshhorn, bronze, 16 × 12 × 12

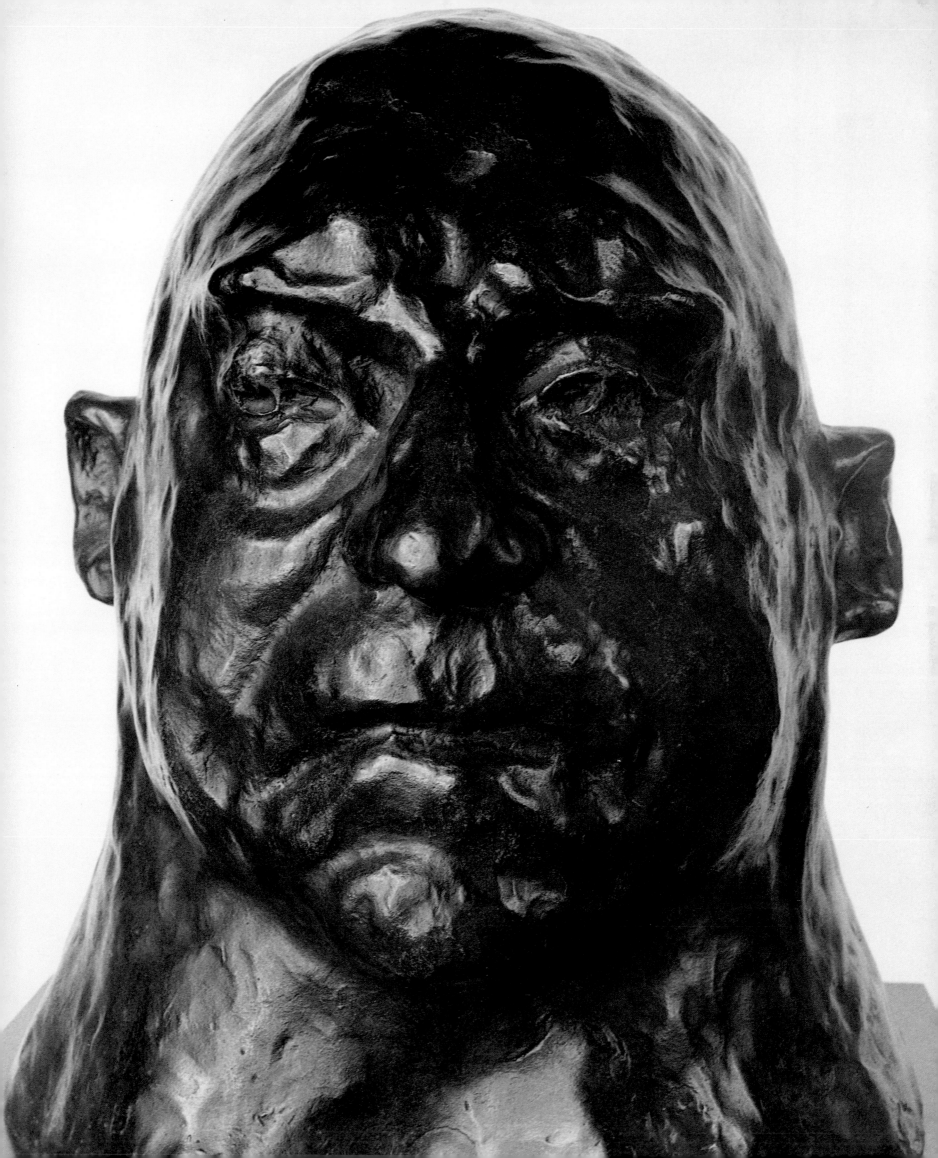

a certain amount of frustration in trying to paint from nature. Natural lighting conditions varied so much, and his free time was limited and at odd hours. He might have an hour or two during the day at one time, or a few free moments late at night at another; light conditions were seldom the same as they were when the picture was started. Quite logically, he turned to sculpture to solve this dilemma and soon found that it suited his life needs exactly. With clay, he could work out a sketchy idea in a few moments and come back to it when the time was available at any hour of the day or night. After the first initial gropings to get the feel of the medium, he began to find his métier, and the work commenced to flow from his fingers. From that beginning in 1951 until the present time—a period spanning thirty years—Nygaard has produced close to eighty sculptures and several hundred drawings.

The social life of the Nygaards was never a busy one because work was always their most important consideration. But there was always time to spend with close friends, such as Trygve Lie and C. J. Hambro and several remarkable people from the world of art. A man very dear and close to Nygaard was the Australian pianist and composer Percy Grainger. The two became acquainted after a Carnegie Hall concert given by Grainger in 1941. Nygaard had always remembered a Grainger concert he had attended when he was a boy in Lillehammer in 1913. At that time the boy had dreams of becoming a concert pianist, and he idolized Grainger. Grainger, in turn, loved everything Nordic and was delighted to find that his music had reached this Norwegian doctor so many years before. In their conversation they found that they both resided in the same town, White Plains, and they naturally arranged a further meeting. This eventually led to the formation of a lasting friendship between the two men. Nygaard has always held Grainger and his art in great respect, and there is little doubt that their close association acted as an encouragement to Nygaard's own reentry into the field of art. Grainger was the kind of artist who felt strongly that the creative forces are a part of all people, and he lived to stimulate these forces in the world around him. In addition to that, he was a very good companion as he was original and unorthodox in his thinking and was vitally interested in a wide range of subjects. Nygaard eventually became his personal physician and remained so to the end of Grainger's life. To this day, he serves on the board of the Percy Grainger Library Society of White Plains: a society dedicated to the preservation of Grainger's home and memorabilia.

Standing Moses, bronze, 7 × 5 × 4
The Virgin Mary, bronze, 11 × 3 × 9, pp. 126, 127

In time Nygaard's circle of friends in art expanded to include such figures in the art world as Marcel Duchamp; Joseph Hirshhorn, the financier and founder of the Hirshhorn Museum of Washington, D.C.; and Alexander Calder. All of these men came to Nygaard through his surgical practice, and all of them came to have appreciation for Nygaard, not only as a surgeon but as an artist as well, and each lent encouragement to his work.

Nygaard was never a member of what is called "the art world": those networks of interlocking associations, ambitions, and influences that are peopled by artists, critics, collectors, dealers, and museum curators. His schedule as a surgeon, his devotion to medicine, and his quiet temperament would never have permitted that possibility. His work in sculpture blossomed within his own quiet environment. The ideas for his work flowed out of his everyday life, out of the knowledge of the world seen from the surgeon's eye, and out of his own inner needs. Time was always a factor that prohibited extraneous activities; it was always a matter of a few minutes here, or an hour or two there, that was best spent with the clay. There was no conflict between his medicine and his art because Nygaard was always first and foremost a medical man who loved his work and gave everything to it. His art was simply another dimension of his life as a surgeon, broadening and enriching its every aspect.

As the years went by and Nygaard became more confident in his ability to create sculpture, he and Ella were able to make several journeys to Europe to visit great museums. These were valuable experiences for Nygaard, as the practice of art always aids the eye to understand more fully what it sees, which in turn inspires the artist to attempt more difficult things. Nygaard's work expanded as a result of these experiences; it became broader in conception and more confident in execution. As his confidence in his ability grew, he began to express his inner ideas more boldly and with more conviction. His personality as an artist began to round out, and gradually his work developed the five general thematic patterns of expression described in the following discussion of specific works.

Hiroshima, painted fiberglass, 56 × 44 × 59, pp. 129, 130, 131
Men Against Man, painted fiberglass, 64 × 54 × 54, pp. 132, 133

Nygaard's Thematic Directions

Since art is itself an explanation in nonverbal, visual terms, any verbal commentary is by its very nature a translation from one sensory realm into another. An artist's work in painting and sculpture usually flows out of the many-layered psychophysical source. This stream of creativity now defines things in one way and in the next moment redefines them in another, always moving in an intangible, living way. These verbal categories are used only to indicate the flows of direction and form his work takes.

INTERPRETATIVE PORTRAITURE

The most universal subject for art (and human attention) is the human head, in particular its hereditary shapes and the modifications of those shapes that have become solidified through the chronic expressions of character. The features of the face represent two coexisting realities at any given moment: one, an emotional history of the person's life and, two, the emotionally layered present state of the person's life. The face is the first thing we attempt to "read" when we meet either an old acquaintance or a total stranger. So it was quite logical that Nygaard was drawn to doing faces when he first attempted to make sculpture in his youth. Also quite naturally, he returned to this mode when he began to do sculpture for the second time in 1951. And he has continued to make sculptures of the human head throughout his whole career. Sometimes these heads are imaginary expressions dealing with specific aspects of human character; others are inner visions of the character of historical, literary, or artistic figures; still others are composite portraits of individuals with whom he is personally acquainted. Though not done directly from life, the portraits of friends are always done in reference to his inner vision and perception of the individual.

Percy Grainger: The Grainger portrait is the third version of Nygaard's loving memorial to his composer friend. It is an above-life-size portrait of a man who, in his talent, his enthusiasms, and his failings, was himself larger than life. There is a strong element of the man as hero. In this portrait's conception, aspects of Grainger's character are conjoined with fleeting expressions of the grief and suffering of this sensitive genius. As in Grainger's own life, his genius, portrayed in this work, seems to transcend self-tormenting drives and to rise above them to achieve victory over inner conflict and self-doubt. There is in this portrait something indomitable and triumphant that emerges, in part from Grainger's own nature and in part from Nygaard's love, understanding, and appreciation for his very difficult and complex friend.

The Death of Savonarola, bronze, 16×34×17, pp. 134, 136, 137
Cancer, bronze, 56×59×22, pp. 138, 139, 140, 141

CANCER

Monument for Knut Hamsun, Norwegian Nobel Prize Winner for Literature, 68 × 72 × 76   143

Marcel Duchamp: This is an astute portrait of one of the most complex and fascinating characters in twentieth-century art. In this portrait, Duchamp's head seems to rise from a vast and long columnar neck; it is as though the head itself were reaching upward to place itself above the world around him. Duchamp's head is drawn slightly backward in an off-balance gesture of chronic reserve and withdrawal. The eyes peer out of the skull with an aloof detachment and wry amusement. The features themselves appear to be pulled backward from confrontation with the world in a noncommital, nonparticipatory expression. In this portrait, Duchamp, the man who left art for chess, is saying "it is your move now, world, but you have lost the game." There is something in the expression of this head that bears a kinship to Samuel Beckett, there is something that says the game of life itself may be at an end. Nygaard's own comment about Duchamp was "he was one of the most cerebral people I've ever met, but very, very charming, not warm or in the least childlike, but very controlled and mystifying." The overall expression of the portrait is that all of the energy in the body is being drawn upward into the head, where it is withheld and converted from action into thought . . . thought not terribly flattering to human existence.

Joseph Hirshhorn: This is a very perceptive study of a genius of finance and the accumulation of wealth, who is also a major art collector and founder of one of the country's most important museums. The head and neck together are almost pyramidal in form; the head rises up from a massive neck and the two form a seemingly immovable unit. The expression of the whole gives an air of unmoving solidity of purpose. The expressions of the facial features are keyed to the mouth, which turns downward at the corners in a stern and unyielding curve. The underlying feeling of the head is that the mouth will not give voice to anything that might be of advantage to any opponent in any transaction. This is a "poker player's" visage, and its expression is enhanced by slight disdain in the curve of the mouth. It gives the impression the opponent's playing is inadequate and the cards are running in Hirshhorn's favor. The eyes alone are mobile, showing a quick and alert expression that sees everything. The eyes are weighing and evaluating instruments, but they are also extremely sensitive to feelings that are seldom expressed, or not expressed directly. This delineation of inner sensitivity and outward unyieldingness provides an interesting insight into Joseph Hirshhorn's two major interests: money and art. The accumulation of wealth is, in psychological terms, the outer self-defensive buffer that protects this man from a hostile world, whereas his inner sensitivity has led him to accumulate art in order to create the Hirshhorn Museum. This portrait is a perceptive study of the

contrasting toughness and gentleness within one human being.
. . . Nygaard's friend Joseph Hirshhorn.

SINGLE SYMBOLIC FIGURES

In his approach to the human figure in its entirety, Nygaard is a symbolist rather than a specialist in the whole range of figurative form, movement, and expression. For him, the figure is a vehicle for the expression of dominant emotions or movements, and these emotions and movements are always suggested rather than modeled in detail. His figures are never done directly from life, nor are they constructed in the Renaissance technique, with exacting proportion and muscular form. They are instead distillations of his own experience and feeling about aspects of life. His figures have more to do with intangibles of mood than with the correct details of living form.

The Surgeon: This work, done in 1956, was Nygaard's first successful full-figure piece. It is a landmark in his development because it is a statement that expresses the emotional and spiritual qualities inherent in the purposes of the profession to which Nygaard has devoted his life. It speaks of the serious responsibilities that are constantly carried by the surgeon in his daily work. It speaks of the surgeon's faith in life quite as much as it speaks of science. It shows the surgeon's vulnerability as well as his strength and the humility before the life force that all physicians must strive to attain.

The Drunkard: This is a relatively early work done in 1958, and it illustrates Nygaard's sense of the figure and its intangible expressions. Though this figure has an awkwardness that is the result of Nygaard's lack of skill in his early struggles with the medium, it has a remarkable expressive presence. The figure is a hauntingly strong aesthetic statement about the difficult human problem of alcoholism. The figure stands in an irresolute stance and seems to waver before our eyes with his right hand thrust awkwardly into his overcoat pocket while the left hand is held furtively behind his back, as though he were trying to hide something. The face of the figure is both a grimace and a leer; it has a look of thirst and secretiveness. Directly behind the figure, and modeled into it, there is another figurative but shadowy presence. What is this indefinable form that haunts and pulls at the figure in the foreground? Is it a personage from the past, a ghost, a demon? Whatever it may be, it is a being who seems to silently guide or control this shell of a human being.

Moses: The *Moses* of Nygaard's late years is a distillation of his feelings about a theme he had dealt with in his first creative surge, when as a youth he painted a picture of *Moses* viewing the Promised Land. *Moses* is an archetypal figure who symbolizes the human concern for lawfulness. Usually *Moses* is por-

trayed as stern and harsh and almost always as unmovingly forceful. Nygaard's Moses is an altogether different conception: The form of Moses rises upward and is itself a mountainlike mass. The instinctive and deeply organic symbolism in Nygaard's form concept is that Moses was himself a mountain of strength and integrity. Rather than being stern, forceful, and forbidding, the expression of Nygaard's Moses is introspectively thoughtful and gracefully capable of movement. The figure also bends slightly to its right with the head turned downward, and the essence of the expression is kindly, warm, and giving . . . within the framework of Moses's inherent power and authority. The modeling of this sculpture is not sophisticated, but the expressive content touches the very core of the subject.

The Virgin Mary: To Nygaard, who is not religious in the formal sense of the word, the figure of the mother of Christ has always held the meaning of being symbolic of the universal maternal spirit of nurturing and compassionate femininity. This sculpture was motivated by a specific experience in Nygaard's life. It was a momentary glimpse of one of his hospital colleagues, a nurse, whom he observed bending over a patient. In that moment, he saw something radiating from her that so moved him he thought about it all day long. When he returned home late that night, he went to his studio and quickly modeled this first version of this figure in a few minutes. This is one of Nygaard's more abstract works, a simple flowing form emerging from the clay. Yet it is a very eloquent expression of his own masculine perception of woman; it is his male response to all that is female in the world, all that is maternal. And here that great gulf between medium and content has been bridged by Nygaard in a single leap: The clay no longer exists . . . only a man's heart speaking!

THE FIGURE GROUPS

Nygaard's figure groups expand his symbolic treatment of the single figure in a logical progression that depicts the symbolic relationships between figures. As a physician, he has come to understand that individuals are not isolated units that act and function without effect on the world around them. He has seen repeatedly that what affects one person will almost always touch others as well: When a loved one dies, something within us also dies; when a loved one is hurt, we are also hurt. Nygaard knows that individuality exists in the same relationship to life as the fish does to the sea, which is to say, . . . man cannot exist without humanity.

Hiroshima . . . the Refugees: The *Hiroshima* sculpture embodies many things from Nygaard's own personal experience and observation of mass human misfortune. The piece is con-

structed of simple and moving forms that blend into a single monolithic shape. From this single shape, a male and a female emerge, both carrying small children in their arms. The work shows them from the waist up, their bodies moving as though they have been caught in a powerful wave. They are of themselves powerless and are swept away by forces far larger than themselves; yet their own energies are concentrated in trying to shield and protect their children. In the content of this sculpture, there is a profound dynamic balance between the figures and the wave that brings a sense of spiritual victory to the fore. The sculpture tells us that the humanity that survives within us, even in disaster, will win out, and that through the instinct for tenderness and nurture, humanity will survive. There is little doubt that Nygaard's early experiences with the refugees of the 1917 Russian Revolution have given some of the emotional charge to this group, or that his work with the Norwegian seamen of World War II has had an influence, but there is also a lifetime of experience that has come from dealing with the human plight of ordinary people in this strangely gentle and hopeful composition.

The piece itself was given important recognition when it won a United Nations competition for works of art dealing with the theme "Refugees" in 1971. The work was reproduced on a United Nations stamp that same year.

Men Against Man: This is a massive composition of peculiar force. Six lumbering and lumpish visor-capped figures in breeches and jackboots carry a single struggling and prostrate figure by force. The willfully ugly movement of blind force of the lumpish figures expresses a mindlessness that is impervious to the humanity of the terrified figure that is held and brutally crushed between these quintessentially obscene totalitarian figures.

This is a work of very rare courage in its delineation of the human ugliness that is inherent in either Red or Black fascism. Nygaard has held nothing back here in his treatment of the effects on mankind of mechanistic state ideology. Here the artist's own lack of technical sophistication is itself utilized as a key expressive device, and it is as though his own moral and spiritual powers have used the very revulsion that these things have created in him to form the clay beneath his hands. Nygaard is telling us the existence of evil is in no way beautiful to look upon. . . . He is telling us that *this* kind of evil is intolerable.

THE ALLEGORICAL SCULPTURES
Nygaard's allegorical sculpture is an extension and variation of his approach to group sculpture that takes a step into more complex symbolic and mythic expressions that emerge from human relationships and historical events.

The Death of Savonarola: This sculpture is a fascinatingly constructed work that was done in 1969. The construction combines an interpretive portrait of Lorenzo de Medici (after that of Verrocchio) with an interpretative portrait of the Borgia pope Alexander VI, both of which are topped off with a wryly conceived nude figure of the hanged Savonarola. All of the figures are skillfully modeled, and the Borgia portrait has some of the same structural devices used in the portrait of Joseph Hirshhorn. Here Nygaard has dealt with a complex historical period that involved forces of power in a counterpoint of violence and reformation. Having been in touch with political personages of power and events of great magnitude in his own life, the artist has brought his experience to bear on this period in the history of Florence with great acumen.

At first glance, the elements of this composition appear to be oddly unrelated, but closer examination shows them to be ingeniously and whimsically integrated into a precarious and rather mad symmetry that is an astute commentary on power politics and the deadly art of political acrobatics. In this work, Nygaard strikes the delicate balance between satire and allegory (with a generous spice of rather wicked wit).

Cancer: The subject of cancer is one few people in art are equipped to deal with. This is true because not much is known about cancer and it is a disease that is frightening to almost everyone. Nygaard is one of those rare people who is capable of dealing with this subject in art because of his great human sensitivity and because he has dealt with it as a surgeon for many years. He understands cancer's effects on the individuals who are afflicted with it; he knows, too, the effects cancer has on those close to the afflicted. Nygaard has experienced the whole range of feelings that emerge from this subject, and he has helped many people to recover from the disease, as well as known those who have been felled by it. The work called *Cancer* is certainly his own tribute and prayer for these people.

In this vision of Nygaard's, a great hand grips a man and a woman in a crushing hold from which there seems no escape. Yet the male figure lifts and bears the weight of the female figure, while the female figure raises her face upward in mute appeal. In the composition, there is a titanic battle of inner forces locked in conflict. The expression of the group is really Nygaard's own voice, and it speaks from his own heart: It says something of what he himself has felt over the years for those he has tried to help. As much as this sculpture does say about the human affliction we know as cancer, it says every bit as much about the nobility of spirit of this artist-surgeon, who lost his own beloved wife to cancer in 1976.

Ambivalence, Edvard Munch, bronze, 20 × 12 × 11, pp. 152, 154, 155
In Memoriam, bronze or fiberglass, 17 × 8½ × 12, pp. 156, 157

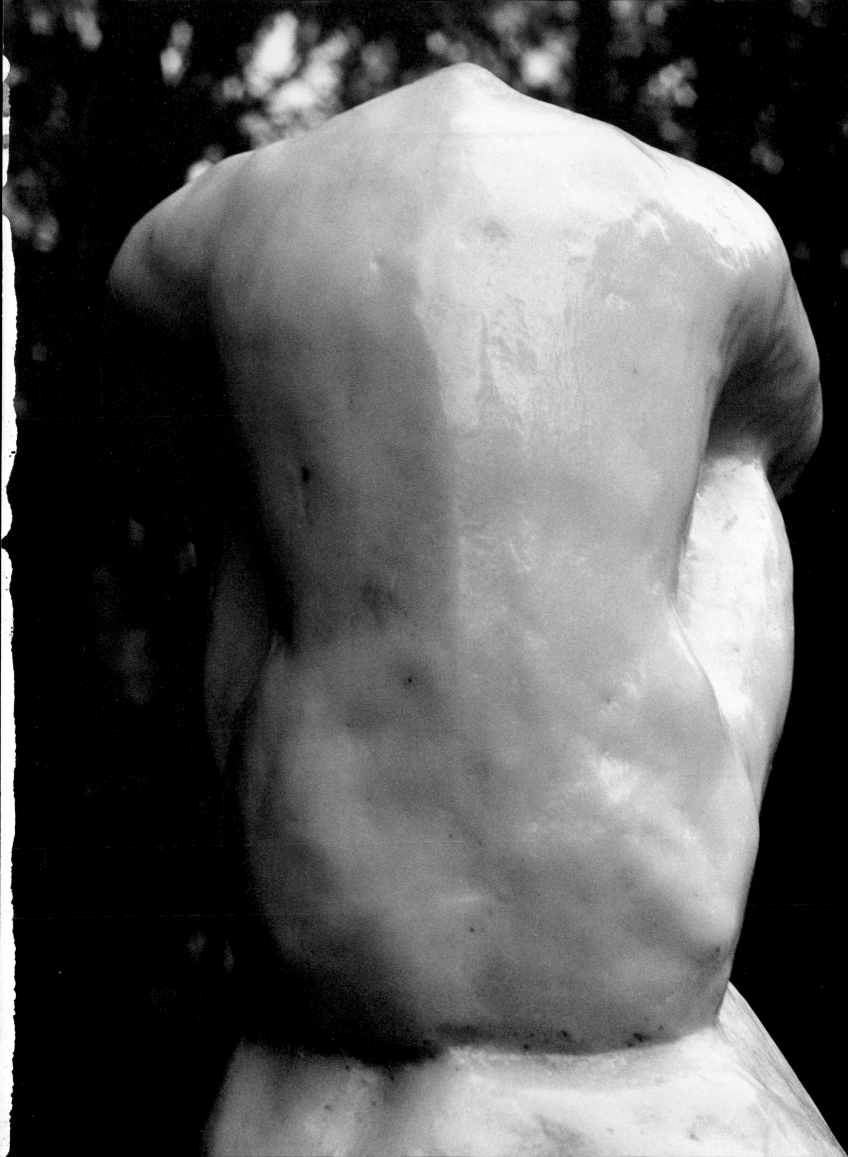

THE PSYCHOLOGICAL STUDIES

The psychological studies of Nygaard are the final expansion of his aesthetic sensibilities. These works utilize his physician's eye in bringing his ultimate aesthetic vision to bear upon the life and character of several great figures from art and literature. These works consist of a skillful montage of forms, expressions, and themes. Nygaard has performed a remarkable synthesis of form in these works that are his most ambitious and most complex.

The Knut Hamsun Sculpture: This is a biographical as well as psychological study of the life and work of the Norwegian literary genius. In this piece, Nygaard interweaves symbolic elements from Hamsun's life with themes from his literary work. The sculpture is built around three large symbolic forms and three subsidiary symbolic figure groupings. The large symbolic forms are a ram's head, which represents Hamsun's rural origin; a great fist, which represents his early protest novels; and a metamorphic portrait of Hamsun in his later years. The subsidiary forms consist of the following: Hamsun as a boy herdsman clinging to the ram's horn at the lower right side of the piece; to the left, behind the fist, are the embracing figures of Johannes and Victoria from Hamsun's early success *Victoria*; and above the ram's head are a group of three figures, all of which are symbolic of Hamsun —on the top, Hamsun the master, lower and to the right is the gaunt figure of Hamsun in his youth when he wrote *Hunger*; on the left is a figure representing the wild elements of Hamsun's genius tamed by the master. A large bronze version of this work has been placed on the Hamsun estate in Norway.

The Munch Sculpture "Ambivalence": Nygaard has titled his study of the Norwegian painter Edvard Munch *Ambivalence* for two reasons: one having to do with the character of Munch himself and the other having to do with the inventive form Nygaard has given to the portrait. From one view, the work represents the head of Munch during his later years. The expression of this head seems at first to be gross and heavy, even arrogant, but closer study discloses a revealing play of emotions on the face of the tormented artist: Munch was born into a brilliant but ailing family and was fearful of insanity and dissolution throughout his life. The reverse side of the head is hollowed out and in the hollowed form are a portrait of Munch as a handsome and sensitive youth and several themes from Munch's famous *Madonna* paintings—the Madonna, the fetus, and forms of the swimming sperm. This is an altogether startling study of Munch that is moving and frightening and arresting in its power and range of emotion.

These five thematic directions of Nygaard's work flow logically out of his own development and are extensions and elaborations of his artistic perceptions and sensibilities.

Wisdom and the Human Image

The work we have been discussing is impressive for many reasons. The work itself represents a remarkable sustained and creative effort that has covered a thirty-year period. In addition to this, these works have been produced by a completely self-taught individual. Nygaard has had no link with any of the schools of the twentieth-century art world or working associations with artistic peers. These works are the children of his inner being, his imagination, and his insight.

The works we see here are this man's own deeply motivated images of emotional importance. There is sound insight in all of Nygaard's work; often there is profound originality, and there is always personal honesty. Nygaard is a man who has experienced life on many profound levels; he is what the French call "un homme serieuse." What we see in his art is the light of his full radiance as a human being. . . . His art cannot be evaluated without sensing his humanity.

We do not have to forgive Nygaard that he did not have the years to spare from his dedication to medicine and human welfare to attend a few drawing classes. Our only responses to Nygaard's artistic strivings are gratitude and appreciation for his creative spirit. Nygaard is our friend and he has striven to tell us valuable things . . . urgent things, vital things . . . and he speaks to us with an honest, visionary, and compassionate heart.

Art in its best sense has never been, and will never be, anything else than human communication. Though at times it may be a cry or a scream, at others it may be a whisper, a warm laugh, or a reassuring word. . . . It is a message from the human soul to the human soul, and no less. Nygaard tells us the serious things he has felt, and he shares with us the wisdom of his life.

Wisdom speaks with its own voice and in its own way. Sometimes the voice is cracked and broken with age, sometimes schooled and sonorous, at other times it is the high piping of the child . . . or even an infant's unformed sounds. But whatever the pitch or timbre of wisdom might be, it is wisdom because of *what* is said. In the art of the human image, we have great need of all the wisdom we can get. When it comes, we must honor what is truly honorable, respect what is truly fine, and revere what is most tenderly human.

K. K. Nygaard, physician, artist to humanity, and Sculptor of the Invisible . . . thank you.

May 1981   Nathan Cabot Hale, Ph. D.
                                             Amenia, New York